$7.95

# The Grand Jury

### The Use and Abuse of Political Power

by Leroy D. Clark
Foreword by Senator Philip A. Hart

*A Publication of the Committee for Public Justice*

The recent actions of the Watergate grand jury, reflecting public outrage, may have obscured the consistent abuse of the grand jury process. Originally conceived to protect the people against arbitrary violation of their rights, the grand jury—especially in the Nixon years—has been subverted in too many instances to an instrument of political harassment.

Although this is a book about law, it is written for the layman. A book about the operation of the grand jury systems faces the danger of being overly narrow in a legalistic sense, but Professor Clark avoids the danger by presenting the history and recent behavior of the grand jury in terms of its potential for political abuse, giving concrete examples and confirming its immediate relevance to all of us. Furthermore, he ties his examples into the overall attitude and practice of the Nixon administration with regard to our legal institutions. This study of the grand jury thus becomes a vehicle for the study of political manipulation of legal institutions with implications beyond the subject on which it is focused.

The author presents, as well, a program for the reform of the grand jury system so that it will better serve a useful and, perhaps, more limited purpose.

# THE
# GRAND
# JURY

LEROY D. CLARK

---

# The Grand Jury

## THE USE AND ABUSE OF POLITICAL POWER

---

*Foreword by*
*Senator Philip A. Hart*

*Quadrangle*
*The New York Times Book Co.*

LIBRARY OF CONGRESS CATALOGING IN PUBLICATION DATA

Clark, Leroy D      1934-

The Grand Jury, the use and abuse of political power.
Includes bibliographical reference and index.
1. Grand jury—United States. I. Title.
KF9642.C45      345'.73'072      72-91377
ISBN 0-8129-0320-X

# CONTENTS

# Acknowledgments

I wish to thank the members of the Committee of Public Justice for asking me to write this book, and especially Norman Dorsen of the New York University Law Faculty, who lent some general comments out of his extensive experience in the civil liberties area that helped set a framework for me. My primary thanks, however, must go to my wife, Christine Philpot Clark, who helped me formulate some of the approaches I took. She and Stephen Gillers edited the entire manuscript, line by line, greatly assisting in making it more readable. Emanuel Geltman of Quadrangle/The New York Times Book Co. made the final and valuable suggestion that I try to place my critique of the grand jury in the context of the events of 1974 concerning Nixon administration officials, which I attempt in the Introduction. The Coalition to end Grand Jury Abuse, especially Fred Solowey, was helpful in providing information on the specific of the abuses of the Grand Jury. The manual prepared for defense lawyers by the Grand Jury Defense Office of the National Lawyers' Guild was also an invaluable aid.

I received excellent research assistance from Arlene Popkin, Gwendolyn Parker, and Yvonne Dixon (the latter especially on the grand jury and newsmen)—which only proved out my evaluation of them as among my best former students.

My two "permanent and rotating" secretaries (only they will know what that means), Kathy Barnier and Olga Hayes, know that my work was greatly facilitated by their competent assistance. Ms. Barnier also pointed out instances where the "legalese" needed to be translated into English. As I neared the finish I received needed secretarial assistance from Dulcie Ingleton and Elizabeth Schuyler, and some helpful comments from my friend from law school days, Sybil Landau.

# FOREWORD

Much time will pass before the nation fully absorbs and recovers from the abuses of power now revealed to have occurred during the Nixon administration. Each revelation, more shocking than the last, rushed upon the public with such rapidity that we have become numbed by the accumulating disclosures. Yet accompanying that numbness is a deep dismay and, for many, despair; Watergate has left behind an unprecedented cynicism and crisis of confidence in government.

Our present chance to help restore that confidence is to study those recent assaults on our political life. We must learn their lessons so that we can fashion safeguards, within the limits of human frailty, against future abuses of the public trust.

It is this task which makes Professor Clark's important work on the American grand jury so timely. He offers a penetrating study of our grand jury system and evaluates its uses and abuses from the nation's birth to yesterday's headlines. Most important is the detailed and documented record he provides of grand jury misuse we have seen in recent years.

The disturbing series of over-reactions to dissent and political opposition might all too easily be forgotten or ignored among the welter of more spectacular events—impeachment proceedings, the resignations of a president and vice president, and notorious trials of other high officials. However, many of the derelictions of the Nixon administration were clearly illegal at the

time they were undertaken; their perpetrators stand charged
with knowing as much. At least in that sense, no matter how re-
pugnant, they present a clear question of whether major reform
of existing legislation is needed. The picture is less clear with
regard to grand jury abuses, as Professor Clark so well demon-
strates. Most of the "abuses" commented on here lie in the gray
ill-defined areas of discretion and action taken with a cloak of
colorable legality.

Clark's central point is an urgent and eloquent plea that the
recent misuse of the grand jury process not be dismissed as a
momentary aberration. Rather, he forces us to view it as illumi-
nating the vulnerability to abuse which permeates the current
system.

The book's historical sweep suggests another factor which
tends to diffuse momentum for reform. Early in our history
grand jury abuse was a matter of seeking ill-founded convictions
of political targets. But more sophisticated modern techniques
now make the grand jury an equally dangerous tool for conducting political surveillance and building dossiers in the guise of
investigating specific offenses. It can also be used simply to harass, intimidate, and disrupt organized political dissent. Therefore, the very small percentage of indictments obtained by the
Internal Security Division of the Justice Department in recent
years which ended in conviction does not reflect the true cost
such abuses may impose upon a free society.

Professor Clark explores a wide variety of proposed changes,
including the alternative, which he rejects, of abolishing the
grand jury completely. Clark's own interesting proposals will be
welcomed by some and heatedly rejected by others, but they
deserve a wide hearing.

Moreover, while he pulls no punches in his case for reform,
his thoughtful analysis fully conveys to the reader the complexity of the issues posed for Congress and the country. Professor
Clark's book will help us refurbish the reputation of an institution which Thomas Jefferson once called the "sacred palladium
of liberty."

                                        Senator Philip A. Hart

# INTRODUCTION

In a time in which public confidence has been put under great stress because some of our most important ex-officials have been given "special dispensations" in subversion of the cherished American principle that the law should be applied uniformly, the federal grand jury seems to have been one small arena in which the phrase "no man is above the law" is still a living reality. As a body of ordinary citizens cloaked with the power to investigate and initiate federal criminal charges, its record for the past few years would seem to be quite impressive. The list of people indicted by the grand jury includes an ex-attorney general of the United States (John N. Mitchell), an ex-secretary of commerce (Maurice Stans), an ex-secretary of the Treasury (John Connally), three men formerly holding the top positions on the White House staff (John W. Dean 3d, John D. Erlichmann, and H. R. Haldeman), and approximately forty-five lesser White House aides and staffers of the Committee for the Re-election of the President. An ex-vice president (Spiro T. Agnew) and another ex-attorney general (Richard G. Kleindienst) have pleaded guilty to some charges under pressure of a grand jury investigation, and a grand jury was ready to name Richard Nixon as a

coconspirator until advised by the special prosecutor that
the Constitution would permit him to be named only as
an "unindicted" coconspirator so long as he held office.
These examples of even-handed justice must have served in
some measure to restore the public's faith in government
after it had been assaulted by the avalanche of disclosures
of criminal activity by high officials—a level of public corruption with no parallel in American history.

To most non-Americans it must seem a very strange
process that permits a group of private citizens to label the
President, the highest public official in the land, as a criminal coconspirator, even if, for technical reasons, no immediate prosecution was authorized. In many other countries, where the top leaders tend to rule more by force
and fiat, their crimes against the society come to light only
*after* they are dead or deposed. Foreign observers in the
more tightly controlled countries, looking on the "strange"
American scene, probably imagined that the widespread
criticism and outright attacks on the major symbol of
authority while he continued to occupy the Presidency
would produce "chaos" in the country (and Nixon composed his variation of this theme by stating indirectly that
charges against him and his practices could harm the
office of the Presidency). Americans, however, regard this
"calling to account" (and rightly so) as a strength of our
particular form of democracy and, indirectly, of course,
of the grand jury—for in most countries there could never
be a wholesale indictment of members of a group then in
power conducted by a group of "mere" citizens.

Not only has the American grand jury traveled the
democratization route in terms of holding the high and
mighty responsible for their offenses, but the base of the
population from which grand jurors are chosen has been
continually broadened. From its early colonial days, when
the membership was drawn solely from white males over

age 21 and, indeed, in many instances only those who owned property, it is now possible, at least according to our formal legislation, for a black female over age 18, who is unemployed but is a registered voter, to sit on the federal grand jury.

With this list of important pluses in favor of the grand jury, it may seem curious (or worse, misguided) that any book would attempt to criticize the federal grand jury as being either outmoded or ill-constructed because of the way in which the Nixon administration was able to use it, when the same institution seems to have operated like an avenging angel to bring a host of charges against many who once held high positions in that administration.

However, before we as a nation applaud ourselves for having processes that rid the body politic of the great abusers of power, and before lauding our institutions for their strength and democratic operation under severe stress, we should look carefully at whether the felicitous results were produced by personalities and fortuitous events, rather than by the institutional structure of the grand jury.

Even though our natural impulse may be to push the painful episodes foisted upon us by our highest officials out of our minds and into history, it is imperative that we stop for a close look at the specific ways and means that they used to jeopardize our liberties. We must be disciplined enough to examine the grand jury, if that was a tool of abuse, and not blithely assume that all is—or was—well because some "name" officials have been called to account by virtue of the operations of that institution. We must ask whether it was the grand jury that was responsible for the recent stunning counterattacks on government corruption and irresponsible use of power, or whether it may have been forces quite independent of the grand jury.

Indeed, the exposure of Watergate and all of the Nixon excesses appears to have been more a product of a number of unusual events, each in part linked to the other, rather than of the existence and actions of the grand jury. The real contributions were the discovery of the burglary of Democratic headquarters by the alertnness of Frank Wills, a black security guard; the arrogance of a President who thought his position so impenetrable that he taped his own criminal conversations; a few crusading, hard-working investigative reporters fueled by an unusually antagonistic relationship between the press and the President, especially that "liberal Eastern" press for whom they worked; and the tough (some would say unconstitutional) sentencing pressure that an indignant and skeptical Judge John T. Sirica put on the Watergate burglars and that finally produced the truth. Indeed, some would say that throughout the whole process the grand jury was characteristically under the control of the prosecutor and functioned adequately or inadequately, depending on which prosecutor was directing it and on what goals he set.

The grand jury's investigation of the Watergate burglary in 1972, led by regular prosecutors from the Justice Department, seemed designed to *deflect* attention from the major culprits in order to get their "boss," the President, beyond the November 1972 elections. These details are presented in Chapter XIX. Only after the appointments of special prosecutors Archibald Cox and Leon Jaworksi were most of the major figures involved indicted by grand juries. These special prosecutors had greater independence from the White House than the regular Justice Department attorneys, a result of much-voiced suspicions by the public and the Congress that previous grand jury investigations had been less than vigorous and complete.

If the grand jury is at all subject to any of the abuses explored herein, we cannot be comforted that it is an instrument that can be wielded for proper law enforcement goals by the "good guys" (in this case, the special prosecutors). It is too risky to rely solely on the electoral process to produce officials who will appoint an attorney general who will utilize the broad powers of the grand jury with restraint and good faith. An institution so deeply concerned with criminal justice should not be so malleable as to be easily turned to illegitimate political ends in the wrong hands. Rather than relying on accidental "good guys," all too rare in the history of any nation, it is the task of law to objectively define limitations on an institution when its operational abuses become apparent—and it is to that end that this book is written.

# THE GRAND JURY

# I.

---

# Prologue: The Shape of the Grand Jury Problem

In the early 1970s, when a few of the more vocal critics of the Nixon administration were crying "creeping fascism" or "police state tactics," most Americans probably thought that this was simply political hysteria and hyperbole. The general belief that we have had, and will always have, an "open" and democratic society is so strong that it is hard for us to take seriously the charge that our government is threatening substantial freedoms and liberties, especially when official power is being wielded quietly and, at least initially, against small groups. However, there are many occasions in our past when those in control have sought their political objectives so intensely that they have subordinated or ignored the question of whether or not the adopted means violated the spirit of our Constitution. The Nixon administration is a study in this kind of failure.

American-style repression usually succeeds by first isolating the target groups from the protection of the courts in that the means of suppression have a surface, or cover, of

"legality." Today we have no overt, publicly approved torture, assassination, or kidnaping for deportation—tactics
used by foreign regimes that make no pretense at being
bound by law or democraitc procedures. But there *are* raids,
unauthorized wiretaps on the offices of unpopular groups in
the name of "national security," or McCarthy-type committees investigating "subversives."

The indifference of the general public to these threats
to civil liberties is assured for differing reasons. Middle-
class status and its accompanying economic well-being have
been sufficiently widespread and continuous in our society
(at least since the 1929 Depression) that, whether one political party is in or out of office or what its respective policies
are while there, are not "survival" issues. Americans seem,
in these terms, apolitical or, rather, nonideological. This
may be positive if it avoids a Chile-type confrontation: One
party will not engage in a *coup d'état* because it has lost
power to the opposition party in an election. However, since
governmental repression is always applied to organized and
highly political people, the average apolitical American,
immediately exempt from such tactics, has little concern or
sympathy for those groups.

The public at large defines its immediate well-being in
terms different from those of activists. For the average
American, consumerism looms larger as an issue of importance than civil liberties. Any group working for change,
however, values its civil liberties highly, for it grants them
the room for action and communication.

Further, perhaps we have become a people who take
our own press release about what a great country this is
too seriously. There is a hidden resentment, especially in
middle America, against change makers who tell us, implicitly, that they are disturbed by the America they see.
Groups trying to act as catalysts are viewed with hostility
for being too helpful to the outgroups (nonwhites, Vietnam-

ese villagers, students, etc.) who we wish would remain invisible and docile while average Americans are getting ahead. They must, after all, get ahead of someone.

The fact that many of the activists come from privileged families, yet evidence a disdain for the very things and values that the average American has worked so hard to achieve, has boomeranged: Their protests against government attempts to suppress outgroups or keep them out disturbs the usual unquestioning public acceptance that what government does is usually right; also, the change makers draw enmity for instilling in the outgroups a sense of belief in their now-common cause. It is these strains that ex-President Nixon tried to pull on and reinforce when he told the "silent majority" of his creation—that he, unlike others, would talk about "those things which are *right* about America."

Against this backdrop of public attitudes, the grand jury was a perfect vehicle for the Nixon administration to use against its political opposition which, while apparently determined and vocal, was always quite limited in number. An institution of legal and historical stature, it existed in England for some 700 years and was inherited during the early Colonial period as a feature of the American legal system. Its repressive potential is disguised by a structure that would appear to be an antidote against arbitrary government action, composed as it is of ordinary citizens from whom a prosecutor must seek approval before another citizen can be prosecuted for a serious crime. Indeed, the Supreme Court has repeatedly said that protection against arbitrary prosecution is its main function:

> Historically, [the grand jury] has been regarded as a primary security for the innocent against hasty, malicious, and oppressive prosecution; it serves the invaluable function in our society of standing between accuser and accused, whether the latter be an individual, minority group,

or whatever, to determine whether a charge is founded
upon reason or was dictated by an intimidating power or
by malice and personal ill will.*

Informed critics now charge, however, that the Nixon administration perverted the grand jury from its historic role
of protection to one of harassment. Specifically, it was actively utilized, illegitimately, as a weapon against a wide
spectrum of people solely because they opposed the policies
of the Nixon administration. There are strong indications
that the Justice Department has used the grand jury to
gather intelligence against groups deemed "radical," to
harass and deplete the resources of political opponents, and
generally to discredit and intimidate people from continuing to support and participate in groups that the administration differs with politically. Hundreds of politically active people have been questioned in grand jury sessions in
great detail about friends and associates; when some have
resisted on the grounds that the federal prosecutor has no
right to penetrate legitimate political organizations, they
have been jailed for contempt. The current charges of abuse
leveled against the federal grand jury, and not the state
bodies, are all the more serious because the federal grand
jury is mandated by the Fifth Amendment of the U.S. Constitution and, thus, cannot be easily dismantled.

*Wood v. Georgia, 370 U.S. 375, 390 (1962).

# II.

----

# The Grand Jury:
# Through the
# Historical Looking
# Glass

What were the historical roots of the grand jury, an institution commanding only hallowed judicial comments? Has it warranted its long-standing reputation as a democratizing and protective agent? Or are there historical antecedents for the current use of the institution as a political weapon?[1]

In an attempt to answer these questions, the establishment of the grand jury in the mid-1100s and the purposes it was designed to achieve must be separated from the character that the grand jury began to develop in the 17th century. Was the grand jury instituted by the English Crown to protect the innocent from unjust prosecution? All historical accounts conclude that it was not. Its creation was the product of a struggle in which Henry II sought to wrest power from the Church and the barons. Soon after Henry II ascended to the throne, he discovered that prior English monarchs had conceded considerable judicial jurisdiction to the ecclesiastical courts. These courts declared the law for wills, marriages, and the inheritance of property. They had complete jurisdiction over any criminal charges against clergy. This state of affairs was particularly galling to the King because for serious offenses, including murder, an accused could claim the "benefit of clergy" and be tried before an ecclesiastical court, where the penalty could be as light as explusion from a Church position. A more compelling reason for Henry II's attempt to recapture judicial control was that the Church reaped significant revenues from fines levied in its courts. Royal warfare required retained mercenaries. Power was dependent on enlarging the sources of income.

In 1164, the Church reluctantly agreed to accept a body that became the earliest forerunner of the modern grand jury. One part of the Constitution of Clarendon abolished the practice of using charges from undisclosed informants as the basis for a bishop's accusation of a layman. Thereafter, an accuser had to make his charges publicly, or, when he was afraid to be the sole public accuser, the sheriff chose twelve men to hear the evidence against the alleged offender and present the charges to the ecclesiastical court.

The criminal jurisdiction of the barons was the next line of attack, undertaken by the King by means of the Assize of Clarendon, issued in 1166. Prior to this move by the King, a lay subject could be privately charged by an injured party before one of the baronial courts. The "trial verdict" depended on either the ability of the accused to find 11 people who would swear to his innocence, or his endurance under trial by battle or ordeal. Under the Assize of Clarendon, the injured party presented evidence before 16 men, who then decided whether the suspect should be accused. Once accused, the suspect was limited to trial by ordeal, for the option of securing 11 men to attest to one's innocence was closed. This panel of 16 men was designed to strengthen the King's control over his subjects, for each juror was expected to bring before the panel people who were under suspicion of criminal misconduct. Thus, the King had, in effect, created a citizens' police force as a means of ensuring central control over criminal prosecution, and one that would generate more charges than the previous system of accusation. An accused did not ordinarily survive the trial by ordeal, which entailed, for example, putting his hand in boiling water and sustaining no injury, or being thrown into a lake and yet managing to avoid drowning without swimming. Thus, the grand jury was greatly feared: Its accusation was tantamount to a verdict of guilt.

To ensure sufficient manpower for the grand jury, heavy fines were levied on those who failed to respond to a summons to serve on a panel. Grand jurors were also penalized if they failed to return an indictment against someone considered indictable by the Crown. They could be fined, too, for failure to make the sufficient number of accusations necessary to keep revenue flowing into the royal treasury. Grand jury duty was considered so onerous that some wealthy landholders secured charters exempting them from serving.

The original functions of an institution can be modified by the development of new and related institutions. By the 17th century, because of two such developments, the grand jury had experienced some reduction in the powerful and central role it had played. First, trial before petit juries began to replace trial by ordeal. The grand jury accusation no longer automatically led to a finding of guilt. Second, Parliament developed, and its taxing power made the grand jury less important as a generator of revenue for the Crown.

The grand jury, however, continued to be the arena for struggles between contending political forces. One such struggle derived from the desire of Charles II of England, the reigning monarch in the latter half of the 17th century, to reestablish the sovereignty of the Catholic Church in that predominately Protestant country. Anthony Ashley Cooper, the first Earl of Shaftesbury, and his follower Stephen Colledge were especially vocal and vigorous in their support for the continued hegemony of the Anglican Church, and they suspected that Charles II did not share this view. A prime concern of the Earl of Shaftesbury was that James, the Duke of York and Charles' brother, also an avowed Roman Catholic, might succeed to the throne. The Earl of Shaftesbury, supported by other members of Parliament, sought to present a bill of indictment to the grand jury alleging that the Duke of York was in violation of laws that required recognition of the Anglican Church. The chief justice of the court, an ally of the King, dismissed the grand jury, thus preventing it from hearing evidence on those charges. The King then countered these tactics by presenting charges to a grand jury in London against Stephen Colledge for allegedly uttering treasonous remarks and plotting his overthrow. The London grand jury refused to indict. Shortly after this attempt against Colledge, the King sought an indictment of Shaftesbury before a London grand jury for treasonous activity, but again the grand jury refused. In this proceeding two important features of the grand jury emerged. The King's counsel sought to hold the grand jury proceeding against Shaftesbury in public, presumably to disgrace him in the eyes of his countrymen. The grand jurors objected, claiming that if grand jury sessions were not secret, suspects would be alerted and would abscond, and suborning of perjury would be facilitated. They also claimed the right to make their decision in private, without outside pressure. Although the chief justice required the hearing to proceed publicly, the grand jury was subsequently lauded by commentators for its effort to establish a tradition of secrecy. The same grand jury sought to resist any domination by

demanding the right to conduct its own questioning of witnesses after the King's counsel finished his interrogation.

The Shaftesbury and Colledge cases are often cited as
the first examples of the independence of the grand jury
from executive pressure. Indeed, it does appear on the surface that citizens sitting on the grand jury protected political
enemies of the Crown from unfounded charges brought by
a hostile government. It is possible, though, that under the
laws of the time there was some basis for the charges against
Shaftesbury and Colledge. The grand jury may not have
been freeing the "innocent"; it was simply a Protestant jury
chosen by Protestant sheriffs, protecting men widely known
to be supporters of the Anglican church.*

Ultimately, the Crown was not prevented from venting
its spleen on its political enemies in these cases; it simply
took the Colledge matter to the town of Oxford, where there
were many supporters of the King. The grand jury there
promptly returned an indictment on less evidence than had
been presented to the one in London. Colledge was tried,
convicted, and executed. (This potential for nullifying one
grand jury's action by reinstituting the matter, without new
evidence, before a different and presumably more "cooperative" grand jury recurs throughout the history of this institution, and the theme has its modern equivalent.)

Shaftesbury himself knew that the happenstance of having grand jurors biased in his favor was crucial if he was
to avoid the fate visited upon Colledge. Accordingly, he fled
into exile upon the election of sheriffs loyal to the King,
who could "pack" the jury with people hostile to him. A
further indication of the Crown's dominance of the grand

---

*However, at the time of the Colledge case one reporter claimed
that the grand jury refused to indict because the charges were
"so notorious a falsehood." G. Burnet, *History of My Own Time*
(1803), p. 504.

jury process was that the foreman of the London grand jury was arrested and later forced to flee the country when he refused to indict Colledge. The King also secured indictments and prosecutions against other members of the Shaftesbury "plot" against him.

This history tends to undercut the claim that the grand jury has always been a strong and independent institution. The grand jury was in existence for five centuries (from the 1160s until the Shaftesbury and Colledge cases in the 1700s) before we have this first instance of its acting as a buffer between the state and the individual. Despite the limited resistance by the grand jurors and their ultimate failure to protect Shaftesbury and Colledge, supporters touted it as an extremely important institution and a key to Englishmen's security. In the 200-year period following the Shaftesbury and Colledge cases, no similar assertions of independence by the grand jury occurred.[2]

# III.

---

# The American Grand Jury: The Colonial and Revolutionary Period

The Englishmen who settled the American colonies established English institutions like the grand jury, albeit with some important modifications that were responsive to the local conditions.[1] The first formal grand jury was established in Massachusetts in 1635, and by 1683 some form of the grand jury was operative in all of the colonies. Grand juries returned indictments for criminal offenses and, quite frequently, presentments, which differed from indictments in that the grand jurors themselves initiated the investigation and could offer any evidence they personally possessed.* The reason that accusations initiated by grand jurors, as opposed to prosecutors, were fairly prevalent (though almost nonexistent today) was early colonial conditions. There was no fully developed police or sheriff force, and the office of

*Presentments subsequently came to signify only noncriminal complaints against public officials, and criminal charges could be proffered only under an indictment prepared by a prosecutor.

prosecutor was also in an embryonic stage. Colonial grand
jurors drawn from the local area often had firsthand knowledge of the particular offense and the alleged offender.
There was nothing like the degree of anonymity and
stranger relationships common to our modern urban cen-
ters. The grand jury, therefore, possessed in fact much of
the autonomy that in theory is supposed to characterize the
institution today.

When grand juries were not particularly active, it was
again due to the stage of colonial development. In the outlying, sparsely settled areas, it was often difficult to find
enough grand jurors. Even where the grand jury was held
in the more populated areas, in the vicinity of the capital of
a colony, it was difficult to get people to attend because
roads were not yet highly developed. Thus, many of the
colonies began to levy fines on the outlying towns that failed
to elect jurymen and on the individual jurists who failed to
attend when chosen.

One of the most interesting innovations in the American colonies, again a by-product of an early stage of development, was the grand jury's adoption of quasi-legislative and
civil watchdog functions. In 1862 in the Carolinas, for example, legislation was promptly considered if it was suggested by a majority of the county grand juries. In a colony
like New York, which had no representative assembly, the
grand jury actually assumed direct ordinance-making powers. Perhaps even more important than these attempts at
influencing legislation were the inspection, investigation,
and complaint functions the grand juries assumed. In some
colonies they inspected bridges, public buildings, and jails
and then issued reports critical of public officials for failure
to construct or operate them properly. The grand jury often
went further and collected taxes, disbursed funds, selected
petit jurors, audited all expenditures of county funds, and
even checked up on people who failed to attend church

regularly. Some grand juries also became a means of publicizing grievances and achieving municipal reforms. One weapon utilized by the grand jury was its report, which sometimes aroused public opinion and stirred officials to action. A town could be prosecuted on a presentment, and matters that were complained of, such as failure to repair streets and roads, were sometimes corrected after a grand jury report. The successful discharge of many of these duties has enhanced the reputation of the grand jury; as we shall see, state grand juries continued to function in much the same manner, although the growth of formal legislatures reduced their scope of operation.

How democratic were these early grand juries in the method of their selection and the breadth of their composition? While Virginia followed the English procedure of having the county sheriff select the grand jury panel, some colonies, such as Massachusetts, elected the grand jurors at town meetings. This democratizing influence, however, was undercut somewhat by the English practice of requiring jurors to own property. While only the Carolinas had formal property qualifications, which were high, elsewhere, where sheriffs chose jurors, the practice was to select landholders, preferably those with sizable holdings. Women (and, obviously, indentured servants and slaves) were not eligible for grand jury service, but these groups did not participate in most of the other formal public life of the early colonies.

Because the grand jury was seen as a powerful institution, those in authority sought to control the selection process so that those chosen would act in compliance with the wishes of the established government. This was, in part, the reason large landholders were chosen by sheriffs for jury service, and why the governor of Virginia directed the sheriffs to select only the "most substantial inhabitants of your counties." The governor of North Carolina dismissed an

uncooperative grand jury, chose one composed of "only
gentlemen of the first rank, property and probity," and was
thus able to secure indictment for violation of the Riot Act
against rebellious colonists in outlying areas of the colony.[2]
In Massachusetts, the Royalist governor restricted the election process in the town meetings by presenting them with
a list of nominees from which the jurors had to be chosen.

The Royalist powers were not able to completely dom-
inate the selection of grand jurors. Thus, the American
colonists gradually recognized the importance of the grand
jury as a direct means of expressing their grievances against
Royalist officials and of blunting the Royalist power to
prosecute by not returning indictments. Colonists were encouraged in this endeavor by the writings of John Somers
and Henry Care in England, which spoke of the importance
of the grand jury as security against malicious prosecution.[3]
These widely distributed writings outlined the powers and
duties of grand juries and were used as a rationale for citizen resistance to Royalist power. The grand jury in the
colony of Georgia, on the basis of these writings, demanded
the right not to specify the particular crime they wished to
investigate but to call before them any person on any
matters they deemed appropriate. (Though an assertion of
independence at the time, it has presented problems in controlling grand juries today). It also resisted an attempt to
disband it, and continued to meet and summon people in
private. A South Carolina grand jury opposed legislation
requiring the confiscation of land for unpaid taxes. The
South Carolina Assembly looked upon this as a signal of
widespread disapproval and refused to pass it.

The reputation of the grand jury as a protector against
government abuse of prosecution persisted in the new American nation in the years just before the Revolution. The
colonial grand juries were prejudiced in favor of smugglers
and others seen as "patriots" opposing British authority.

Where the colonists had some form of local representative government, they passed legislation barring initiation of prosecution based solely on the royal prosecutor's information. This was done precisely to force resort to the colonial grand jury, which would not indict those with whom it was in political sympathy. Grand juries played a key role as the opposition to British authority became more overt. In 1765, Boston grand jurors refused to return an indictment against those accused of leading the Stamp Act Riots. Grand juries ignored chief justices who exhorted them to enforce the law to avoid "mob rule": One group refused to take the oath and sit where one chief justice was thought to be a puppet of the Royalists because, under new legislation, he received his salary from the Crown. Finally, the English, to regain control over the grand juries, tried to abolish the elective grand jury in Massachusetts, but the colonists continued to elect their own grand jurors. The sheriffs were supposed to choose more compliant jurors under this British legislation, but public pressure forced them not to carry out their duties.

As the dispute with Britain headed toward open conflict, the grand juries issued reports charging the British with "oppression." Judges sympathetic to the colonies used the grand jury as a forum in which to voice support for the developing resistance to British rule. When war broke out, the juries returned treason indictments against colonists who sided with the British. People sympathetic to the Crown were, naturally, disqualified from service on the grand juries.

From this pre-Revolutionary and Revolutionary period, the grand jury received much of the esteem that now attaches to the institution; however, it did not function in any strict sense to protect the "innocent" against arbitrary and unfounded prosecution. Much of the colonialists' activity, such as burning tea chests brought to the colonies by the

British ships in 1774, was blatantly illegal, yet the grand jury blocked charges brought against the participants. Indeed, some participants in the protest action sat on the grand jury that heard the matter. The local grand jury that indicted British soldiers who fired on colonialists in the Boston Massacre of March 1770 may also have indicted four civilians who were completely innocent but were suspected of being British sympathizers. The only evidence that the grand jury did protect the innocent was its refusal, in 1768, to indict the editors of the Boston *Gazette* for allegedly libeling the Royalist governor, and its refusal (twice) in 1735, to indict John Peter Zenger for seditious libel of the Royal governor of New York. These prosecutions seem to have been arbitrary and calculated attempts to harass and silence the political opposition, although, as in the Shaftesbury and Colledge cases, it is possible that these writers had technically violated British law as it stood at that time. The total evidence indicates that the grand jury did not operate to check corrupt and arbitrary administration of the criminal law by nullifying politically motivated prosecutions but, rather, that it was an instrument for denunciation of, resistance to, and ultimately, warfare against British authorities.*

---

*After the Revolution, when the patriotic fever had abated, grand juries do seem to have restrained some vindictive prosecutions against people who were accused by various committees of being British sympathizers.

# IV.

---

## The Grand Jury
## in the New Nation:
## Did It Fulfill
## Its Promise?

However much, in hindsight, the grand jury of the pre-Revolutionary and Revolutionary period did not fit the ideal now extolled in statements by appellate courts, it was a highly esteemed institution when the colonies formed themselves into a nation. After 1776, it was included in many state constitutions, and the Fifth Amendment to the U.S. Constitution assured that any serious federal criminal charge would be screened by a grand jury.* The federal Constitution's provisions were adopted not only because the grand jury had a key role in the Revolution but also because

*The Amendment reads: "No person shall be held to answer for a capital, or otherwise infamous crime, unless on a presentment or indictment of a Grand Jury, except in cases arising in the land or naval forces, or in the Militia, when in actual service in time of War or public danger . . ."

many colonists were fearful of creating a powerful central government that could arbitrarily use the criminal process against its political enemies.

In retrospect, did the grand jury become the shield that it was proposed to be, to protect the innocent against abuse of the criminal charge and deprivation of liberty? The sad fact is that, by and large, unless a defendant could pass a "popularity test"—that is, unless the local populace favored him or his activity, he stood little chance of being protected against unfounded accusations. And conversely, if the defendant was popular, he would not be indicted even if the evidence of his guilt was overwhelming. The grand jury never developed fully into a consistent "neutral" institution, scrupulously sifting the evidence and providing protection only for the innocent. It frequently reflected local or prevailing prejudices in the decision to indict or not to indict.

Shortly after the new nation was formed, a sharp political division developed between those grouped around John Adams, the "Federalists," and those allied with Thomas Jefferson, the Republicans or "Anti-Federalists." The Federalists supported a strong central government and opposed the libertarian and egalitarian notions that emanated from the French Revolution. The Republicans tended to take the opposite view. When the Federalists were in control of the government, the Anti-Federalists charged they were using partisan federal grand juries to indict people under the new Sedition Act solely because they spoke out against the party in power. The grand jury cannot be blamed entirely for the ease with which the Republican opposition was harassed, for Federalist judges were improperly pressuring them by giving intemperate charges. Also, it may have been easy to bring charges under sedition laws that were especially broad and inclusive, making illegal almost any vigorous criticism of government.* There was some basis for the Republican claim of bias, however, because the indictments all occurred in the New England and Mid-Atlantic states, which were Federalist strongholds where grand jurors were likely to be hostile to defendants of the Republican persuasion.

One might have imagined that when the Republicans came to office in 1800 they would have been constrained by their own previous rhetoric against unfair use of the grand jury against one's political enemies, but this was not so. Thomas Jefferson had spoken of the grand jury as a "sacred palladium of liberty,"[1] but his administration tried repeatedly to indict Aaron Burr solely because of political differences. It finally succeeded in Virginia, a state with strong loyalties to Jefferson. Burr was ultimately acquitted of the treason charge, and at least one historian has concluded that it was preposterous that he was even indicted, given the insufficiency of the evidence.[2] Even the grand juries that refused to indict Burr may not have paid attention to the insufficiency of the evidence, for they were predominantly Republicans who had an animus against the Federalist attorney who was conducting the grand jury sessions.

Grand juries, which had resisted enforcement of unpopular legislation, simply carried that practice over to the post-Revolutionary period. When indictments were sought for violations of the Neutrality Acts of 1793, grand jurors who were sympathetic to the recruitment of men and outfitting of ships for the aid of France refused to indict. The

*Politics*

*Politica*

---

*The sedition laws punished any "persons who combined to oppose any measures of government to impede the operation of laws, to intimidate officers of the United States in the discharge of their duties to defame the government, Congress or the President." Alien and Sedition Law of 1798, Chapter 74, Sections 1-4, Stat. 596.

admonitions of federal judges that refusal to enforce legislation was no longer an act of patriotism went unheeded.

The biased or partisan grand jury was not limited to this early period in American history. In the 1850s, when Mormons dominated the grand juries in Utah, they refused to charge church members with polygamy or for violently resisting federal troops and non-Mormon settlers in their territories. Conversely, they indicted some non-Mormon judges for alleged crimes whenever those judges criticized the Mormon Church and its customs.

Although most grand jury action around the slave question in pre-Civil War days occurred in the South, the Federalist judiciary in Boston, which wanted to placate the South, was unsuccessful in its first try to indict Theodore Parker, who had urged the forcible rescue of a runaway slave in the custody of federal marshals. (It must be remembered that Boston was the heart of antislavery activity.) A second attempt to indict was successful when a relative of the presiding judge sat on the grand jury and was alleged to have exercised substantial influence on other members. Only in the northern abolitionist states were some individuals indicted for kidnaping free blacks in order to sell them back into slavery. Kidnapings also occurred in the South, and while grand juries sometimes "protested," there is no record of anyone being indicted for such conduct.

In 1842, when blacks in Philadelphia were celebrating the abolition of slavery in the British West Indies, a crowd of whites tried to break up the parade, and fights ensued. Whites later went through the black section of town stoning and beating people and burning down a newly constructed black church. The grand jury that investigated the matter indicted no whites and placed the blame on the black community for "undue provocation."[3]

Southern grand juries were especially aggressive in the enforcement of the slave codes and laws placing restrictions on free blacks. People were charged with inciting slaves to rebellion when they appeared only to have made speeches to other whites attacking slavery as cruel and inhuman. The grand jury also interrogated postmasters in order to prevent antislavery literature from coming into their states.

During the War Between the States, northern grand juries publicly rebuked newspapers that appeared to support the southern position, resulting in their being banned from the mails by federal authorities. The activity of the newspapers, however, was obviously not sufficient "aid and comfort" to the enemy to result in a criminal indictment.

After the war, when the federal government sought indictment against people in the South who violated the Ku Klux Klan Act or other federal measures to protect blacks, people who supported the southern rebellion were excluded from grand jury duty to avoid complete nullification of the protective legislation. The state grand juries, which did not exclude people who supported the old Confederacy, regularly failed to indict for Klan activity even when blacks had been kidnaped, maimed, or lynched.

The grand juries in more recent times have continued to reflect responsiveness to local or national bias, or to executive pressure that labels one or another group as "dangerous" and deserving of indictment. When President Franklin D. Roosevelt became incensed by Nazi propagandists who attacked his leadership in the early 1940s, his attorney general, who doubted the legality of the sedition charges, found no difficulty in getting a grand jury to return an indictment at a time when patriotism was an intense and unquestioned feeling.

In 1948, when the public was gripped with fear of the Communist party (much of it generated by the executive branch as it fought the cold war), a grand jury in New York readily indicted party officials for violation of the Smith Act, which prohibited advocating and teaching the legitimacy of overthrowing the government. This may be no evidence of any active bias, for grand jurors may not be equipped or authorized to raise serious questions about the constitutionality of a given law, or to refuse to indict on that basis. However, an index of the strong reaction was that one grand jury was not content simply with the indictments but also issued a report complaining that more indictments could not be secured because alleged members of the party were invoking the protections of the Fifth Amendment. Another grand jury denounced the State Department for giving United Nations clearance to people believed to have had some leftist affiliations in the past.

In Denver and Los Angeles grand juries began to call members of the Communist party, and the ensuing events parallel much of what, as we shall see, occurred with grand juries in the 1970s. Witnesses were told that there were no charges against them and that being a member of the Communist party was not a crime. When some of them invoked their privilege not to incriminate themselves, citing the fact that members of the party had been indicted two months previously in New York under the Smith Act, the court disallowed their claim and they were imprisoned for contempt. (The same witnesses *were* in fact later indicted under the Smith Act, proving that their claim of the privilege was well founded.)

Some witnesses were ordered to appear before the grand jury on three hours' notice. During contempt proceedings witnesses were put in custody overnight and denied time with their attorneys for needed consultation. Some witnesses released on bail pending appeal of their contempt sentences were immediately called back to the same grand jury for further questioning. Upon refusal to answer in the second round, they were found guilty of criminal contempt and sentenced to one year. The grand jury investigations were conducted concurrently with widely publicized hearings into "subversive" activity by the House Un-American Activities Committee. It has been claimed that one purpose of the committee investigation was to create a cloud of suspicion around officials of the United Electrical Radio and Machine Workers of America, who were suspected of leftist sympathies, in the hope that their membership would defect to a new union sponsored by the CIO.*

## AN EVALUATION OF HISTORICAL MATERIAL

How is this history of the grand jury pertinent to a study of contemporary abuses of the grand jury? Has an institution that has been included in the Bill of Rights and that continues to exist in some states any valuable functions to perform?

The history we have surveyed, admittedly selective, does not exhaust the examples of grand juries' failing in their protective function. Still, grand juries, at both the federal and state levels, probably operate properly when dealing with routine matters. This is so because a prosecutor normally has no interest in bringing weak cases before the grand jury. With strong cases, the jury's function will simply to validate a reasonable discretionary judgment.**

*These grand jury investigations have been detailed by one of the counsel for defendants, Leonard Boudin, in "The Constitutional Privilege in Operation"—12 Lawyers Guild Review 128 (1952). In conversations with the author, Mr. Boudin claimed that he had tried to get major bar associations to look into the questions concerning interference with the lawyer-client relationship, to no avail.

**It has been claimed that a prosecutor might bring a weak case before the grand jury when he does not want to take the responsibility for the decision not to prosecute. For example, when there may be criminal charges against a police officer, the D.A. may welcome another agency's throwing the case out so that it cannot be said that he was in league with the police department to let its men escape responsibility for criminal acts.

The selected history, however, does show that in periods of severe political stress, or when a locality or the nation has been caught up in some intense ideological struggle, the grand jurors have shared the political sympathies of the prosecuting agent, and unpopular accused people have not been protected against improper or politically inspired charges. It is important to note these failures, for the grand jury is still an institution spoken of reverently by our highest courts.* Also, we should be more ready to entertain reform if it can be shown that current civil liberty abuses have some historical antecedents and are a product of how the institution has been structured over the past 200 years.

Some of the deviations of the grand jury from optimal performance could be defended as nothing more than the excesses we can expect from an institution that is "democratic" and, therefore, reflective of intense local concerns. In this guise, it is a kind of "people's court" that we indirectly authorize to break the law when some current and local interests are strongly felt. The southern grand juries that reinforced slavery and resisted reconstruction were not pursuing goals that we approve of today, but they were achieving the goals supported by the overwhelming majority of the (white) population. Perhaps strong, local community sentiment should always be able to determine whether a law should or should not be enforced under particular circumstances. However, we should be explicit and clear that *that* is the goal we are setting for the grand jury. It is clearly *not* the most idealized goal of shielding innocent, albeit unpopular, persons from arbitrary govern-

*The first crack in the adulation has come as recent grand jury litigation has reached the courts at an accelerated pace. See *U.S. v. Dionisio,* in which Justice Stewart noted that "the Grand Jury may not always serve its historic role as a protective bulwark standing solidly between the ordinary citizen and an overzealous prosecutor." 93 S. Ct. 764, 773 (1973).

mental action that, historically and currently, we have said that the grand jury should be pursuing.

When we ask what positive functions the grand jury has displayed, we must distinguish between the state and the federal grand jury. My primary concern here is to assess the value and strength of the federal grand jury, since most of the current claims of abuses of civil liberties are directed at the national investigating and indicting machinery.

The scope of state grand juries is much broader than that of the federal in that they are authorized to investigate any criminal matter that violates the common law, including typical offenses such as murder, burglary, and robbery. Since the federal grand jury could indict only for offenses of federal law, it had a limited scope of operation until Congress began to pass more federal statutes.

Another feature that distinguished the state from the federal grand jury was that the former continued the colonial practice of being roving investigators who reprimanded local officials, made complaints and grievances, and even suggested new legislation. This is significant, since a major claim for the importance of the grand jury is that it gives the average citizen an impact on governmental operations outside the formal election process. Because the federal government was more remote from the federal grand juries and it was generally thought that federal grand juries were empowered to investigate and indict for statutory offenses only, they were not as accessible as a point where pressure could be applied by lay citizens on the operations of the federal government.* The federal grand jury, therefore, became primarily an instrument for prosecution by a centralized administration.

*In Chapter XIV I will explore the possibility of grand jury reports in the impeachment context. Chapter XVI covers new legislation that explicitly authorizes some grand jury reports on local crime conditions.

The need for federal *and* state grand juries as catalysts
for "reform" has been greatly reduced by the growth of
other groups that can perform this function more efficiently.
The federal grand jury that investigated the Watergate
scandal returned criminal indictments, but the Senate Select Committee on Presidential Campaign Activities (Senate Watergate Committee), chaired by Senator Sam Ervin,
made its primary focus the reform of the executive branch
in order to deter a repetition of the abuses of the democratic
process that had been uncovered. Also, since the Committee,
unlike the grand jury, can conduct open hearings, it can
better publicize the problems and generate the public concern essential for reform. Federal legislative committees
also are not limited to investigations of criminal activity.
They can call experts to suggest solutions to the problems
the committee is studying. One might fear that the honesty
and thoroughness of an investigation may be compromised
if one government official is investigating another, especially, as with the Ervin Committee, when the investigated
and some of the investigators are members of the same
political party. The outrage, indignation, and disinterest
that the average citizen could bring may be lost. This criticism is valid, but there are now well-conceived citizen protest organizations, such as Ralph Nader's organization,
Common Cause, and others, that can provide this monitoring function and the needed independence. Such groups
also have the benefit of choosing people who are informed
on the problem under investigation, unlike grand jurors,
who are randomly chosen. They do not have a fixed period
within which to operate, and can hire a staff of experts or
spend time acquiring expertise. It is true that they do not
have subpoena power to compel people to submit evidence,
but much of the information needed to support demands
for reform is available and simply requires collection and

analysis to point out institutional malfunctioning.* Thus, the grand jury, especially at the federal level, has been eclipsed as an important device for citizen complaint against inefficiency and lapse in government operations.

Equal to the grand jury's reputation as a protector of the innocent and a citizen watchdog committee is its reputation as an effective crime fighter. Thomas Dewey, who had utilized the grand jury effectively in his racket-busting activity, as governor of New York vetoed legislation that would have curtailed the scope of the state grand jury. He said that grand juries were "the bulwark of protection for the innocent and the sword of the community against wrong-doers."[4] State grand juries had a well-earned reputation for exposing municipal corruption. In some instances they depended on the cooperation of the local county prosecutor, but sometimes the local prosecuting attorney sought to stifle the investigation, especially when there was some suspicion that he, himself, was involved in the local corruption. In these instances the grand juries of the late 1800s asserted an independence that is rarely seen today. When the grand jury, for example, began to investigate the corrupt Tweed Ring in New York City in 1872, it did so without the assistance of experts from the district attorney's office. The grand jurors constituted themselves into committees and went out to interview potential witnesses. In their off-duty hours they secured some evidence of fraudulent activity, and they subsequently indicted the mayor, Tweed, and other members of the ring. Similar action was taken by a New York City grand jury in 1900. When the district attorney seemed reluctant to investigate gambling and graft, the jurors simply began to subpoena witnesses on their own, refusing to go through his office. In 1902,

*At the federal level, for example, the Freedom of Information Act has given citizen groups greater access to government records.

grand jurors in Minneapolis went so far as to hire their own private detectives to assist them in securing evidence after the county prosecutor refused to cooperate.

Vigorous attacks on public officials involved in corruption took place in Cincinnati, Chicago, Milwaukee, Minneapolis, San Francisco, and St. Louis between 1870 and 1920. It is to be noted, however, that all of these examples of assertion of independence occurred almost exclusively with state, and not federal, grand juries and involved acting against the government, not ordinary citizens. This fact may inform us of the arena in which the grand jury is most effective.

Federal grand juries were especially active in bringing antitrust charges against large businesses. Such activity, however, was not generally undertaken independently by grand jurors, but was instituted and led by the federal prosecutor. There are few instances of federal grand juries' circumventing federal prosecutors or asserting the same kind of independence sometimes shown by state grand juries.

The passivity of the federal grand jury, as currently structured, is not surprising when one looks at the tasks they perform. Corruption in local government, which the state grand juries have combated somewhat successfully, is more apt to be focused on by local citizens, especially if they are aided, as they often are, by a crusading newspaper. Further, the kind of crimes that are controlled primarily by the state are ones that are most understood by local citizens, such as bribery, murder, theft, and robbery. At the federal level, grand juries may be called upon to investigate highly complicated securities and exchange frauds whose legal basis the average layman is unlikely to understand. Such offenses require preliminary and extensive investigation by a prosecutor before the matter can be brought before a grand jury.

# V.

---

# Politicizing the Department of Justice

The grand jury's reputation and potential as a crime fighter made it a natural weapon for the Nixon administration, which came to office on a promise of "law and order" as the centerpiece of its campaign strategy. While in 1968 many individuals and some groups saw extrication from the Vietnam War as the paramount national problem and wished the issue to be central in the presidential campaign, the Nixon strategy was designed to downgrade the war and keep statements on it fairly ambiguous. Thus, candidate Nixon informed the country that he had "a secret plan" for ending the war. Since negotiations were then under way, active discussion by the candidates could only harm the prospects for final peace.

The crime issue, by comparison, was worked to near-demagogic proportions. As many commentators have noted, it is strange for candidates for federal office to focus on crime, especially "street crime," since the prosecution of most crimes is, under the Constitution, a power solely of the states and not of the federal government. It is true, however, that the direction and tone of the U.S. Justice Department could be a model, or set a style, for local law enforcement offices. Thus, Nixon promised the country a new attorney general who would, presumably, be "tougher" on criminal elements. Aside from the serious problems that can be created by misleading the public with inflated campaign rhetoric, it is not illegitimate for a new administration to try a more vigorous (if even-handed) enforcement of the law.

There were early hints, though, that the Justice Department was not to be a neutral law enforcement agency but, instead, responsive to the interests of the White House, and that its arsenal of weapons, including the grand jury, would be used against those whom the Nixon administration believed to be in political opposition.[1] The transcripts of White House tapes that were forced from Nixon in 1974 show that he explicitly considered the use of the FBI and the Justice Department in this manner. As early as 1968, Nixon is reported to have said at a private meeting of Republicans prior to his election that he was personally going to "take charge" of the Justice Department and run it.[2] He chose perhaps his best prosecutorial alter ego in order to achieve that goal when he made John Mitchell attorney general. Mitchell had been his law partner, close personal associate, and former campaign manager, and, during his tenure as attorney general, claimed to have almost daily contact with the President. Some have called this arrangement good and necessary. Others have strenuously opposed any active, regular intervention by the President, since as an elected official he brings primarily political considerations to bear, causing impartial law enforcement to suffer. The solution is admittedly a difficult one, for the President is obviously responsible for the general policy developed by the executive branch; law enforcement is clearly one way in which this policy is concretely manifested.[3]

Millions of crimes are committed each year. Law enforcement cannot reach every technical infraction. Decisions have to be made about how limited resources will be deployed. Even with these qualifications, law enforcement should be as neutral as possible because it performs a crucial stabilizing function. Stability is lost if one faction uses law enforcement to attack another and if people are subjected to (or are free from) criminal prosecution solely because Democrats or Republicans are in office. No abrupt and temporal shifts should occur each time a new President is elected. The antitrust laws are spoken of as the prime example of an occasion for presidential intervention because breaking up large businesses or suppressing monopolistic practices can have a substantial impact on the economy. (It is, probably, for precisely this reason that criminal prosecution is a clumsy tool in this area and other mechanisms that permit planning and better control ought to be employed.)

If a President disagrees strongly with the particular provisions of or the policy underlying a given criminal law, it behooves him to seek congressional repeal or modification of that legislation. It should be outside the bounds of discretion to direct the attorney general to subvert the legislation by nonenforcement. Conversely, the Justice Department should not adopt strained or "surprise" interpretations of current criminal law to prosecute particular behavior that may not be expressly prohibited. The latter probably occurred when Mitchell decided to prosecute the 1968 Chicago demonstrators for conspiracy to riot even after Ramsey Clark, his predecessor, had studied the situation and decided that there was no basis for prosecution. This also happened in the Pentagon Papers case, which, as we shall see, involved many challenges to the manner in which the grand jury was used. The Pentagon Papers case never reached the jury, but we now know that jurors in the Chicago case apparently agreed with Clark.

Other administrations may, like the Nixon administration, have been guilty of insufficiently insulating the Justice Department from the primarily political and electoral considerations of officials in the White House. Like Nixon, John Kennedy chose his campaign manager, Robert Kennedy, to be attorney general.* Some may be ready to overlook the political uses of the Justice Department under Kennedy because the protection of the law was being accorded to those engaged in civil rights activity in the South or because the Justice Department was mobilizing its resources against men with unsavory racket reputations, like James Hoffa. However, it is dangerous to have law enforcement turn primarily on concern for the black vote, the liberal vote, or the animus of an attorney general for one or another person.

As difficult as it is to resolve some of the problems of intermingling executive policy with law enforcement, it is fairly clear that the Nixon administration took a qualitative leap when it sought to use the coercive tools of the criminal process against critics who were simply exercising their lawful right to dissent.

Nixon has always implicitly adopted the stance that he spoke from some fixed, true American position and that those in opposition to his conservative views were not engaged in healthy criticism but were, either directly or indirectly, disloyal to established government. Not only did he surround himself with close aides who echoed this theme, but the two key men he chose to shape the policies of the Justice Department, John Mitchell and then Deputy Attorney General (later Attorney General) Richard Kleindienst, also shared this view. A classic example of John

---

*Presidents Warren G. Harding, Harry Truman, and Dwight D. Eisenhower also appointed their campaign managers to the position of attorney general. A number of proposals have recently been made to prevent this practice in the future.

Mitchell's overreaction (or planned reaction) to Americans' exercising their right to dissent was his directive ordering wholesale arrests of demonstrators (and/or innocent bystanders as well) who marched on the Pentagon in 1969 to protest against our involvement in the Vietnam War. Kleindienst, for his part, had promised to crack down on "anarchistic kids" and "militants" with the full force of the Justice Department.* Thus, the stage was set for men with a hard line and a narrow view of political dissent to utilize the full repressive potential of the Justice Department and the grand jury.

A program of suppressing dissent, however, can be carried out only if the public or Congress is in the mood to support it, or at least to remain silent or indifferent. This was the mood of the country when Nixon assumed the Presidency in 1969.

The history of the grand jury shows that grand jurors will support indictment as a weapon against so-called "enemies" of the government if the public from which they are drawn perceives the accused similarly. The public that Nixon confronted as he took office in his first term had been propagandized by a virulent attack on leftists during the 1950s McCarthy era. While many liberals now deplore the excesses of that period of political witch hunting, all too many were silent for fear of being investigated themselves or of being considered "fellow travelers," or else because they did not perceive serious and long-range dangers to political heterodoxy. Thus, there was no serious, active op-

---

*Richard Harris, *Justice, The Crisis of Law, Order and Freedom in America*, p. 135. Kleindienst is also reported to have said that politicizing the Justice Department was inevitable and not "undesirable," because "in every Presidential campaign there are big issues relating to law. You can't say after the election that the President should turn the Justice Department over to some computer for the pristine pure purpose of enforcing the law."

position to the scare tactics adopted by rightists and to the serious threat to civil liberties. Few stood up and challenged frontally the thesis that a totally infiltrated, small group of leftists was a dangerous conspiracy that had serious potential for overthrowing the American government. The labeling of the Communist party and other leftists as criminal and dangerous probably still grips the public mind. It is not a long step to take, especially by a person like Nixon, who actively supported the McCarthy campaign, to assimilate the "New Left" in the public mind with the image of the old left as a group of plotting subversives.

Also, by 1968 the American public seemed confused and frightened by the numerous and "extreme" types of political and social crises that had occurred during the previous decade, from assassinations of major public figures, including a President, a presidential candidate, and two black leaders of national and international repute, to explosions in the black ghettos summer after summer, beginning with Watts in 1964. The average American, equating patriotism with unquestioning allegiance to the government's foreign policy, was probably shocked by the depth of the only broadly based and vigorous dissent to a foreign war in American history,[4] especially when that dissent took the form of demonstrations, which occasionally ended in fights between demonstrators and the police, open calls for violation of the draft law, and some, although sporadic, terrorism and bombing. The civil liberties of any small group may be easily threatened when the larger public is fearful and apprehensive about the mode of the dissent and public officials seek to focus the fear on the dissenting group as "rotten apples" responsible for all the anxiety. Concern for the propriety and legality of the means used to reduce the perceived danger becomes minimized to the point of non-existence in the haste to pursue "safety."

The First Amendment expressly prohibits Congress

from "abridging the freedom of speech, or of the press; or the right of the people peaceably to assemble, and to petition the Government for a redress of grievances." Discomforting as the notion of dissent (and all the basic disagreement and continuing campaigning it implies) may be, this nation was founded firmly for and on the protection of that right. The First Amendment is in fact the *first* Amendment, evidencing the priority it had for the creators of our Constitution.

Somehow, the years of post-World War II affluence and the complacency of the 1950s, frequently eulogized and satirized in the arts, lulled the national consciousness into an apparent assurance that all was well for everybody. When sure and noisy groups let the word go forth that it was not so, the majority, for whom most matters had gone better than expected, was at first surprised, then shocked, then resentful. It rejected the "revisionist" contention that America had many deprived citizens.

It was against this background that America needed Nixon; it was more than symbolic that he had been a member of the House Un-American Activities Committee during the McCarthy era and that his vice presidency occupied most of the 1950s.

Dissent, at best, seemed dangerous. The tone of those times controlled the national consciousness to a far greater extent than the high-sounding principles of centuries earlier, which had protected some vague, historical value called the right to dissent. Social dislocations did not quite fit in Civics 101.

# VI.

---

# The Wiretap Legislation: Prelude to Grand Jury Surveillance of the "Disloyal Opposition"

The Nixon administration not only had a public eager for the "law and order" motif, but a Congress as well, which in its "followship" role passed some legislation affecting the grand jury that had strong repressive potential. The grand jury legislation was sponsored and demanded by Nixon's attorney general, John Mitchell, and Congressmen with an anxious eye on reelection could hardly have it said that they had voted against anything that could be labeled "anti-crime" legislation. In that kind of atmosphere, though, legislation may not be as effective as it is claimed to be in achieving crime control.

For example, the provisions in the Omnibus Crime Control and Safe Streets Act of 1968 authorizing the federal and state governments to wiretap suspected criminals were proposed because of their supposed usefulness in fighting organized crime. Major crime figures know that the FBI has identified the leadership of the major crime rings. Since they also know that the new legislation gives the police access to their telephones, they will, when possible, find other means of communicating. It has certainly been the pattern of organized crime to make defensive adjustments to any change in law enforcement techniques. On the other hand, since the authority for wiretapping included crimes like rioting, which is hardly an activity in which organized crime participates, wiretapping could, as Watergate with its subsequent "White House horrors" has shown, be abused to invade any citizen's privacy and to keep political critics of administration policy under surveillance.

Ramsey Clark, Attorney General during Lyndon Johnson's administration, had opposed the use of wiretapping, except in matters concerning the national security, because of its inherent potential for invading the privacy of totally innocent people who might speak on a tapped phone about their own lawful and personal matters. He even closely scrutinized the requests for national security wiretaps and is reported to have taken the unusual step of denying the request when it did not appear to be absolutely necessary. (The need for such control, even when there is an alleged national security interest, is illustrated by the wiretapping of Dr. Martin Luther King. There is some dispute about who requested the King tap, but it was probably either Robert Kennedy, when he was attorney general, or J. Edgar Hoover, then FBI director. In any event, it proves how vague and undefined the concept of "national security" is if it allows a tap on an apostle of nonviolence who preached a doctrine that ultimately only ensured domestic security.)

The attitude of John Mitchell on wiretaps reveals the premises on which he thought the Justice Department and the executive branch could operate, and makes more understandable the particular manner in which the grand jury was used during his tenure in office. After some of the public and visible actors in the demonstrations at the 1968 Democratic Convention in Chicago had been indicted for conspiracy to incite a riot, the Justice Department revealed that it had wiretaps on some demonstrators and that none of the wiretaps had been authorized by a federal court. Mitchell made the claim, for the first time in open litigation, that in matters that the executive branch unilaterally defined as touching on "national security" it could wiretap anyone for as long as it chose to do so, and that court approval was not required. The American Civil Liberties Union promptly brought suit to challenge this position, and the Supreme Court flatly rejected Mitchell's claim.* But these claims illustrate the Nixon–Mitchell view that executive and prosecutorial agencies can operate unfettered by any standards or screening measures required by the judiciary.

The decision declaring warrantless wiretaps illegal was a serious blow to Mitchell's Justice Department, since it invalidated a favorite weapon against the administration's most vigorous opposition. Public disclosures about the surveillance of well-known liberals, whose only error appears to have been insufficient enthusiasm for Nixon as President, have provoked headlines. But many people to the left of the liberal establishment who are not "names," such as the Socialist Workers party and the Young Socialist Alliance, have been subjected to illegal surveillance for years, be-

---

*United States v. United States District Court, 407 U.S. 297 (1972).

ginning before the time of the Nixon administration.[1] The cases in which such wiretapping has been discovered are legion, and one wonders how many have not yet come to light. To name only a few that we know of: the Vietnam Veterans against the War and their counsel, who were prosecuted in Gainsville, Florida; associates of Daniel and Philip Berrigan and the Catholic left; the national offices of the Students for a Democratic Society (SDS) in Chicago during 1969 and 1970; and David Hilliard, an officer of the Black Panther party.

# VII.

---

How to Launder
a Wiretap—or,
Getting More
Mileage out of the
Grand Jury

The Justice Department, unsuccessful in getting approval
to use warrantless wiretaps directly as evidence, resorted to
the grand jury to use the illegal wiretaps indirectly. The key
to this approach is that, as the law stands, a defendant
cannot object to evidence because it was seized in violation
of the constitutional rights of another person. The defendant can only object to evidence seized in violation of *his
own* constitutional rights.* To capitalize on this state of the
law, the government had to find a way to get witnesses,
whose privacy *had* been invaded by an illegal tap, to testify
and give it evidence against another targeted defendant.
The grand jury was chosen as the means by which to ac-

*Alderman v. United States,* 394 U.S. 165 (1969).

complish this goal. The case the government sought to build against Catholic leftists in early 1971 in Harrisburg, Pennsylvania, is a good illustration of this design.

Sisters Joques Egan and Pat Chanel were subpoenaed in a grand jury investigation of the alleged plot by members of the Catholic left to kidnap Henry Kissinger and blow up underground electrical conduits and steampipes near the Capitol buildings in Washington, D.C. They refused to testify, even after receiving immunity against prosecution. They claimed that they could not be compelled to answer questions that were based on illegal information acquired with electronic surveillance or wiretapping. They were cited for contempt and ordered imprisoned. On appeal, the government argued that it had no obligation to admit or deny that it was questioning these two witnesses on the basis of what it had obtained through illegal surveillance. It argued that the grand jury had special, broad powers of investigation and could demand testimony irrespective of whether it was derived by unlawfully invading the privacy of the subpoenaed witness at some time in the past. The government also said that Egan and Chanel would not be injured by their own testimony inasmuch as their privacy had already been invaded; thus, the only protection they could now demand was freedom from prosecution, and they were given that by a grant of immunity. If such illegal invasions of a witness' privacy could be used to aid the prosecution of another person, this would definitely have encouraged future use of the practice.

The government did not win, but whether it succeeded depends on whether "success" is measured from a formal legal standpoint or on the basis of the practices that could be adopted in ordinary cases in the future. The Supreme Court, by the slimmest margin (five to four), held that a witness could not be convicted of contempt when the government refused to deny that its lines of questioning were initially based on illegal wiretapping.*

The decision, however, did not hinge on protecting the constitutional rights or privacy of the witness (as Justice Douglas claimed it should have), but rested primarily on statutory grounds. Thus, the decision preventing the invasion of privacy in order to produce grand jury evidence could be changed by Congress if it saw the Court's interpretation as hindering grand jury investigations.

The *Egan* and *Chanel* cases are special and may not tell us whether the grand jury will be used as a cover for illegal wiretapping in the future. Government exploitation of the illegal evidence was unsuccessful in those cases because Egan and Chanel were closely and intensely aligned with the potential targets of the investigation. They objected to the questioning partly out of religious conviction and also out of a commonly shared opposition to the Vietnam War. Thus, they would readily court imprisonment while they challenged the legality of their questioning. Others, without these incentives, may be easier prey for the government. Since it may take a high degree of personal commitment (and resources) to assert the right not to testify after being illegally tapped, the government may still, in the future, be able to force a few associates to inform on the political activity of key activists whose ideas and programs the government regards with disfavor.

*United States v. Gelbhard*, 408 U.S. 41 (1972).

# VIII.

---

## Using the Grand Jury to Gather Intelligence on Political Dissidents

Since the grand jury is designed for, and may even be limited to, investigations of criminal activity, it should be primarily an instrument to look *back* at past events in gathering evidence to prove prior offenses. It can also look at any current ongoing criminal schemes; it is not, in theory or purpose, supposed to be a data- or intelligence-gathering mechanism, especially if the government's only purpose is to keep an eye on its lawful political opposition. The ability to have meetings, groups, and associations without government interference is a precondition for citizen action and impact on government. Once a group knows that it is under surveillance by law enforcement officials and that records are kept on its activities, its effectiveness is inhibited, if not totally destroyed. Furthermore, such citizens are never aware of how or when the government will use the information it has gathered; government disapproval, either overt or covert, can block a citizen from enjoying important opportunities or benefits (e.g., government appointment, employment, or grants).

Many court decisions—some, we will see, recently won by the Nixon administration—have heightened the potential for using the grand jury primarily for gathering information about critics of the government and not simply to win indictments. These decisions have given almost unlimited scope to grand jury investigations. A grand jury investigation "may be triggered by tips, rumors, evidence, . . . or the personal knowledge of the grand jurors."* The witness cannot object to the materiality or relevance of any questions. Indeed, in most instances such objections are impossible, for nothing has to be disclosed to a witness or the prime target, not even the nature of the charges being investigated. Even in the rare instances in which a suspect discovers the laws under which he will be charged, he cannot, prior to indictment, test their constitutionality and thus preclude being indicted, arrested, and forced to trial.

Open and unlimited probing is possible, in part, because most rules of evidence that normally protect a defendant in a criminal trial, such as the barring of hearsay or irrelevant and prejudicial evidence, need not be observed in the grand jury proceeding. The courts' explanation for the lack of limitations on these forays is that the grand jury is engaged primarily in protecting the innocent, a notion that, as we have seen, is belied by history. Some cases say that, at a minimum, since grand juries are an appendage or arm of the court, they have no broader scope of investigation than the criminal jurisdiction of that court. Thus, investigation into a citizen's personal affairs or associations, unrelated to ferreting out evidence of a crime, should

---

*Costello v. United States,* 350 U.S. 359, 362 (1955).

strictly be improper. However, because the witness is not informed about the purpose of the investigation, and because courts assume that all prosecutions are *ab initio* conducted in good faith, the grand jury is, as a practical matter, unrestrained.

The extensive questioning about witnesses' personal habits and group affiliations support fears that the Justice Department under John Mitchell sought to exploit the broad discretion granted the grand jury in order to gather intelligence on political activists.[1] A grand jury convened in Tuscon, Arizona, in the fall of 1970 was among the first governmental probings of this sort. The ostensible subject of the investigation was the purchase of dynamite by John Fuerst, later identified as a Weatherman. A woman (Teri Volpin), who owned the car that Fuerst was allegedly driving, and four people who lived with her were kept under surveillance by the FBI for several months. The FBI learned that they were living in a commune and were members of a radical community in southern California. They were all subpoenaed by the Tucson grand jury. It is not a usual practice to call the real target of a potential indictment before the grand jury if the prosecutor wishes to avoid the possibility of the suspect's absconding. Therefore, these people were probably sought only as witnesses. The following, however, indicates the type of questioning to which they were subjected:

> Tell the grand jury, please, where you were employed during the year 1970, by whom you were employed during the year 1970, how long you have been so employed and what the amount of remuneration for your employment has been during the year 1970.
>
> Tell the grand jury every place you went after you returned to your apartment from Cuba, every city you visited, with whom and by what means of transportation you traveled and who you visited at all of the places you

went during the times of your travels after you left your apartment in Ann Arbor, Michigan, in May of 1970.

I want you to describe for the grand jury every occasion during the year 1970, when you have been in contact with, attended meetings which were conducted by, or attended by, or been any place when any individual spoke whom you knew to be associated with or affiliated with Students for a Democratic Society, the Weathermen, the Communist party or any other organization advocating revolutionary overthrow of the United States, describing for the grand jury when these incidents occurred, where they occurred, who was present and what was said by all persons there and what you did at the time that you were in these meetings, groups, associations or conversations.

It is unlikely that a court would enjoin the prosecutor from continuing this line of questioning, however much it only seeks to chart the movement and membership of radical groups, for the prosecutor will always ask some questions that appear relevant to the investigation of specific criminal charges, such as, here, the inquiry about the Weatherman organization, or some other questions that were asked of the owner of the car about its use.

Use of the grand jury as part of an intelligence network is not likely to be apparent to a court in any given case; a judge would have to see the full mosaic of grand jury operations across the country and note the pressures put on lawyers chosen by radicals, some of whom have themselves been called before grand juries.

One feature giving credence to the belief that a centrally directed plan was at work is that these grand jury investigations were supervised primarily by the Internal Security Division (ISD) of the Justice Department. Initially set up under Attorney General Brownell in the 1950s and waning at the end of the McCarthy era, this unit was reinvigorated in December 1970 by a staff increase of 1000 per cent, from 6 to 60 lawyers.* Robert Mardian, former general counsel of HEW and a conservative on civil rights issues, was made head of the unit.** He chose Guy Goodwin, an ex-Democrat from Wichita, Kansas, to head the special litigation section.

Goodwin regularly left Washington, D.C., traveling about the country to personally conduct seventeen grand jury investigations. He was chief prosecutor for the Tucson, Seattle, and Harrisburg grand jury investigations, and personally accounted for approximately one-fourth of the indictments secured. He was fond of displaying his intimate knowledge of the New Left in the grand jury room. Goodwin was personally present (unusual for a prosecutor) to arrest a group who had invaded a selective service office in Camden, N.J. in August 1971, and took delight in addressing each by his most common nickname.

Contrary to the usual practice, in which local federal prosecutors investigate and prosecute matters that arise in their districts, ISD has kept control over these grand jury investigations, although they have occurred in 36 states and 84 cities. This kind of centralization is consonant with a plan to implement a national strategy. The claim that ISD central control is for "efficiency" when the cases are brought to trial is not borne out by the facts. On the primary measurement of efficiency, namely, successful prosecutions, the ISD grand juries have not been very good. Although at least 100 separate grand jury investigations have been conducted by ISD, calling 1000 to 2000 witnesses over a three-year period,[2] only 10 per cent of the approximately 200 indict-

*The unit was renamed the Internal Security Section in 1973 and placed under the Criminal Division of the Justice Department, but it continued its grand jury activity.

**Mardian subsequently pleaded guilty to perjury during the Watergate scandals.

ments that have come to trial have resulted in convictions.[3]
The rest have resulted in acquittals or, occasionally, dismissals, as in Detroit, when Judge Damon Keith ordered the
government to disclose the extent of its warrantless wiretaps. The government decided, instead, to drop the charges.
(The conviction rate in ordinary cases is about 65.2 per
cent.)[4]

### THE LAWYER AS A SOURCE OF INFORMATION

The intelligence-gathering thrust of the unit is evidenced
by the fact that Mardian was also given control over the
Interdivisional Intelligence Unit, as investigative department whose primary targets were SDS, the Black Panthers,
the Weathermen, and the other aggressive groups challenging the usual tenets of the political status quo.

The testimony of John W. Dean 3rd, former counsel
to the White House, and documents submitted by him to
the Senate Select Committee on Presidential Campaign
Activities show that the security chief of the Committee for
the Re-election of the President, James McCord, had regular resort to the supposedly highly restricted ISD intelligence files. There are approximately 15 reported occasions
on which lawyers representing radical groups have had their
offices broken into or set on fire between 1970 and 1973.
While there is no hard evidence to identify the perpetrators, McCord, it will be remembered, was convicted for
being a part of the Watergate burglary, and people high up
in the Nixon administration, like Charles Colson, had authorized similar burglaries (i.e., the office of Daniel Ellsberg's psychiatrist). The office break-ins often did not appear to be the work of common thieves because items like
typewriters or, occasionally, money in plain view were not
stolen. But the files of activist clients were rifled or taken.

# IX.

---

# Jail for "Noncooperation" (Putting Radicals on Ice)

Jailing witnesses, either for contempt, under the "material witness" statutes, or by setting a witness up for perjury charges, seems a collaterial goal of ISD in its handling of grand juries. Approximately 30 people have been held in contempt, and 21 have been imprisoned by grand juries conducted under the unit's supervision.*

Leslie Bacon was one, and her case shows that the grand jury is utilized not only as an information-gathering mechanism but also for making an "example" of a political activist by setting her up for contempt charges. This grand jury was convened in Seattle immediately following the Tucson investigation. Bacon was active in the planned anti-war protest to be conducted by the May Day Organization in the summer of 1971. On April 27, 1971, she was arrested in

---

*Paul Cowan, "The New Grand Jury—A Kind of Immunity That Leads to Jail," *The New York Times Magazine,* April 29, 1973. Cowan notes 30 people as having been cited for contempt.

Washington, D.C., as a material witness and held under $100,000 bail because of an alleged intention to flee. She was flown to Seattle, and reports were leaked to the press that made it appear that she was involved in the bombing in the Capitol in Washington, D.C., on March 1.

The prosecutor first learned, through his grand jury questioning, that she had been in radical communities in Greenwich Village, the East Village, Boston, Buffalo, Washington, D.C., and California. He then asked her in great detail about visits that appeared to be only social, asking how many people were with her, what conversations she had in a car during a 56-hour drive, and who slept with whom in what specific rooms in the houses of friends she visited.

Bacon, though only 19 years old, had a wide acquaintanceship in radical circles. Initially, she was advised by a lawyer not yet alerted to the style of these political grand juries, and she testified freely. When a new lawyer entered the situation, he counseled her to take the Fifth Amendment. When she balked at further questioning, the court held her in contempt on the ground that she had waived her privilege against self-incrimination because she had already begun to discuss the subject matter of the interrogation. As a further punitive measure against her for refusing to testify, the federal prosecutor conducting the grand jury proceeding tried to get the Manhattan district attorney to reinstitute investigation into her involvement in a bank bombing plot there, even though a previous state grand jury had refused to indict her on that charge. When this effort failed, the FBI itself issued a warrant for her arrest, charging a federal crime of interstate conspiracy to bomb the bank. That these governmental pursuits were merely abusive and for information-gathering purposes was indicated in a subsequent appellate court ruling that the government had no evidence whatsoever supporting its claim that Bacon had to be held in custody as a material witness to secure her testimony. Finally, the charges with respect to the conspiracy against the bank were never prosecuted because the government refused to disclose its use of illegal wiretaps.

At the urging of John Mitchell's Department of Justice, Congress strengthened the statutory bases for harassment of certain witnesses by enacting the portions of the Organized Crime Control Act of 1970 that regulate granting witnesses immunity from prosecution when giving grand jury testimony. Prior to this legislation, if a prosecutor wanted a witness to give testimony that could be evidence against the witness in a criminal prosecution, he had to offer him "transactional" immunity in order to compel the testimony, which means that the witness could not be charged with any offense about which he was questioned. The 1970 legislation, however, cut back on this by establishing "use" immunity, which provides much less protection: The prosecution is only barred from using the witness's testimony in later attempts to develop evidence to prove any offense the witness is charged with, but the witness may be prosecuted on offenses about which he has been compelled to testify. A witness who is tried at a future date then has the highly difficult task of rebutting the prosecutor's claims that the evidence used against him at trial was not derived, directly or indirectly, from his testimony before the grand jury. Even though the court places the initial burden on the prosecutor to prove that there was no use of the testimony, the witness will rarely be able to counter any of its denials of improper use, since he is not privy to the internal operation of the prosecutor's office. Moreover, even if one assumes good faith on the part of the prosecutor, as a practical matter it is almost impossible for a prosecutor to know whether some one of his associates, or an agent investigating the charges, has, in some manner, improperly used grand jury testimony. If we presume that the witness is likely to be highly reluctant to rely on the good faith of the prosecutor, we then have the spectacle of a witness who is ordinarily free from any possible imprisonment winding up being jailed for contempt because he distrusts the future intentions or ability of the Justice Department to keep its promises. Government duplicity and outright lying became such regular phenomena during the Johnson and Nixon administrations that many citizens doubt the integrity of the prosecutor's office because it is a part of the executive branch.

But the Supreme Court has said that the "use" immunity statutes do *not* violate the Constitution. Five Irish-Americans (Kenneth Terney, Thomas Laffey, Matthias Reilly, Paschal Morahan, and Daniel Crawford) might have gone to jail because they believed that their testimony could be used in a future prosecution against them. They were subpoenaed from New York City to testify in Fort Worth, Texas, before a grand jury investigating the possible shipment of arms from this country to the Irish Republican Army in Northern Ireland. The five charged that the investigation was politically inspired and that they were subjected to harassment because the Nixon administration was creating an appearance of concern for its ally, Britain, in response to its problems with Northern Ireland. They all refused to testify, claiming that their right not to incriminate themselves would be violated in view of the inability of the U.S. government to stop the British government from using their testimony in a prosecution in England. (Some were British citizens.) They were, thus, claiming that even transactional immunity, in the context of possible foreign prosecution, was not full protection. They were imprisoned for contempt for most of a 10-month period.* The court responded that there were various mechanisms that would protect the witnesses against foreign prosecution, including the secrecy of grand jury investigations and *in camera* proceedings if the testimony became the subject of future litigation. It was very clear, however, that if the secrecy of the proceedings were at all breached—a not unlikely event—and the material were indeed secured by a foreign country, the United States had no power to prevent the use of the evidence against those individuals in such a prosecution.

There have often been leaks from the grand jury about testimony supposedly given in secret, as we will see. One matter that might easily escape attention is that all five men *may* have been totally innocent of *any* actual involvement in gunrunning themselves. Simply being called before a grand jury is no evidence of guilt—most people called are simply witnesses and never become defendants—nor is the invocation of the Fifth Amendment against self-incrimination synonymous with an admission of guilt. Invoking the amendment is an assertion of the right, guaranteed under the Constitution, to remain silent rather than give coerced testimony that could be used as evidence against oneself in a criminal prosecution. It is a right that even the innocent have—not to give evidence that might make one *look* as if he were guilty. It can be asserted on a principled basis that *any* compelled testimony is a violation of this privilege. (At least one Supreme Court justice has consistently maintained just that.)** Obviously, the government did not have any

---

*The five were released twice for brief periods on bond by Justice Douglas, pending review by the full court of legal questions they raised.

**J. Douglas, *Ullman v. United States,* 350 U.S. 422, at 446 (1956) (dissenting).

independent information to warrant an arrest and charge
any of the five men for gunrunning because the extensive
penalties applicable to that offense would have more effectively encouraged their cooperation than the 18-month
sentence available for contempt. Proof that the government
imprisoned them solely for refusing to testify is the fact
that they were released from prison in November 1973,
when the grand jury term expired; not one, however, has
been charged with the gunrunning offenses allegedly under
investigation. The more likely explanation of the refusal of
these men to testify is their belief that the real target of the
Nixon administration was the group whose cause they believed in, the Irish Northern Aid Society; thus, they refused
to make openings for any attack on that organization.

# X.

---

Disruption of
the Groups — The
Government Goal;
Organized
Resistance — The
Response

It has been charged that the ISD-supervised grand jury investigations were not initiated solely to gather intelligence or to jail people for contempt, but were part of a broader plan to disrupt the cohesiveness of groups by generating internal fear, thus preventing them from being effective in opposing government policies.

The intimidation of lawyers for political activists has entailed, in addition to the crude rifling of their files, subpoenaing them before grand juries in connection with people they were representing or had represented in the past.* In the fall of 1970, Arthur Kinoy, well known among radicals as an attorney who will come to their aid, was subpoenaed to testify as to the whereabouts of his daughter Joanne. Kinoy sought to stop the subpoena by asserting that calling him before the grand jury would undermine the belief among the unpopular groups he represented that confidences disclosed to him as their attorney would be protected, that he had represented his daughter in the past in civil rights cases, and that he conceived of himself as in an attorney-client relationship with her. The court ruled against him on all points, claiming that he could protect the attorney-client relationship by refusing to answer any question put to him in the grand jury that intruded on that relationship, but that he could not claim a right not to appear at all. The court also found that his knowledge of his daughter's whereabouts was derived not from attorney-client communications but from his parental relationship. Although a husband and wife have the privilege of not testifying against one another, the court said that none existed to protect the relationship between father and daughter (or, as Daniel Ellsberg was to learn, between father and son).[1] Mr. Kinoy was spared contempt charges because his daughter subsequently appeared and was subpoenaed for grand jury inquiry.

The same tactic was used against Sanford M. Katz and Gerald B. Lefcourt, at one time members of a New York law commune, who represented members of the Black Panther organization and other radical groups. They were summoned before the grand jury to disclose who had retained them to represent a particular defendant, the address of

*This tactic parallels the practice in the 1950s of calling the attorneys of people under investigation for alleged subversive activity, in addition to their clients, before the House Un-American Activities Committee.

that person, who had promised to pay their fee, and whether one of the defendants to the conspiracy charge who had retained them earlier was, in fact, the party who had arranged for them to represent that defendant. The court temporarily released them from the subpoena because it saw that this could, potentially, be a way to gather evidence for a pending indictment. (There is a rule against using the grand jury to pile up proof to be used at trial after it has handed down an indictment, but the prosecutor can always claim that fresh offenses of defendants are being pursued. The courts have no way to evaluate those claims; thus, the rule is easily circumvented.) The protection against their summoning lawyers in this instance, however, was not given a firm constitutional basis—such as finding the inquiry to be a violation of a defendant's right to counsel. Indeed, the court said that the inquiry of the lawyers could be resumed after disposing of the pending indictments against their clients.

A court may be loath to openly label a prosecutor's tactic coercive because of its strict requirements of proof and because of the tradition of deference to other branches of government, but it is easy to understand that calling an attorney into secret sessions of the grand jury is apt to create a great sense of vulnerability, particularly in groups that perceive the government as hostile to them and their ideas. They will not be able to predict how much the confidentiality of the attorney-client relationship can be penetrated. The lawyer may find himself in the strange position of having to retain another lawyer to interpret to his clients the scope of the inquiry. Given the almost unlimited reach of grand jury interrogation, the attorney will be hard pressed to convince his clients that confidential communications will be protected, especially if the client himself has been subjected to sweeping grand jury questioning. Groups that

have formerly seen their lawyer as the last shield against
arbitrary jailing may truncate their disclosures to him—thus
undermining his capacity to defend them.

Unmistakable evidence that governmental surveillance
had the further purpose of "freezing" group protest
emerged when the papers stolen by the Committee to Investigate the FBI from the FBI office in Media, Pennsylvania, were released. These papers indicated that about 40
per cent of the agency's time was spent spying on old-line
civil rights organizations and new antiwar groups. One of
the memos taken concerned New Left groups and informed
all agents that at an FBI conference held at headquarters in
September 1970:

> there was a pretty general consensus that more interviews
> with these subjects and hangers-on are in order for plenty
> of reasons, chief of which are it will enhance the paranoia
> endemic in these circles and will further serve to get the
> point across there is an FBI agent behind every mailbox.[2]

At attempt to frighten off financial supporters from as
aboveboard an activity as placing an advertisement in a
newspaper could be gleaned from one grand jury investigation. A group calling itself the International Committee to
Defend Eldridge Cleaver took out an ad in *The New York
Times* in November 1968 to raise funds to support his
legal defense against what they claimed were violations of
his constitutional rights. In 1969, after Nixon came to office,
the grand jury subpoenaed Sandra Levinson and Nathan
Schwerner under a claim that it was investigating "mail
fraud." The government initially sought documents with
the names of contributors to the Committee and volunteer
workers. This was an old tactic that the Supreme Court
had invalidated when southern states tried to compel civil
rights organizations to produce their membership lists—

with the obvious purpose of discouraging people fearing reprisals from joining those organizations.* When Levinson and Schwerner appealed, the government dropped this demand. The district court, however, permitted the grand jury to inquire into the disposition of collected funds without any prior showing by the prosecutor that he had some evidence of mail fraud.** Even though no indictment resulted, the group could have difficulty in the future retaining contributors who may have developed doubts about their *bona fides* simply because the investigation was begun.

A witness before a grand jury can have other problems maintaining the confidence of his political associates. Testimony given in secret may generate fear and suspicion among them, because those not present cannot know what is being disclosed. This is true even if the group is not engaged in criminal activities for which they fear prosecution. They may believe the government wants information on their legitimate lawful activities in order to thwart or neutralize their programs. ISD, perhaps knowing that secret testimony has that impact, has resisted efforts by witnesses to get transcripts of their testimony. A witness does not violate grand jury secrecy by speaking about his own testimony, but obviously, a transcript would create more confidence among others. One court may have been sensitive to this, because it refused to hold Anthony Russo, a friend of Daniel Ellsberg, in contempt unless he was given a copy of his testimony.[3]

The alternative the witness has is to refuse to testify about any of his associations, group activity, or personal

*Gibson v. Florida Legislative Investigation Committee,* 372 U.S. 539 (1963).

**Levinson v. Attorney General of the United States,* 321 F. Supp. 984 (1970).

movements and thereby accept imprisonment if he is
granted immunity from prosecution. It may seem unreasonable for a person to maintain loyalty to a group and refuse
to testify solely on the basis of suspicion by the government, especially when he does not believe he will incriminate himself or others. However, resisting authority that is
regarded as unjust and arbitrary has become common on
the American scene in the past fifteen years of intense civil
rights and antiwar protest. Such resistance has been especially intense when young people have felt that the government was intruding on their new life style of communes,
underground newspapers, draft counseling, and other activities not generally engaged in by nine-to-fivers. (ISD,
for example, subpoenaed more than 100 people in the California area who sought or dispensed draft counseling.)[4]

Resistance to the ISD grand jury began to escalate and develop a loose organizational character. The Coalition to End
Grand Jury Abuse, spearheaded by Fred Solowey, was set up
to educate the public and develop model legislation. It was
endorsed by the ACLU, National Conference of Black Lawyers, National Emergency Civil Liberties Committee, and
the Unitarian Universalist Association. A grand jury defense office, sponsored by the National Lawyers Guild, was
organized. It pulled together an excellent manual to quickly
alert attorneys as to the law and strategies possible in grand
jury defense, and also supplied attorneys for witnesses. Un-
degeround newspapers began to alert their readership to the
new grand jury strategy. Local defense committees were
formed in twelve cities to deal with the problem of individuals' being picked up and isolated from group support.
After the Bacon case, they met and formed a loosely knit
organization called Non-Collaboration. It called for resistance to the grand jury on moral grounds and in the name
of group unity. The following, put out by the Bay Area

Committee to Stop the Grand Jury, is an example of the strong stand of member groups:

> some people up before this grand jury are going to talk. we don't recommend it. you can be indicted for anything they ask you about, even if you've been granted bullshit "use immunity." you can be indicted for perjury. you can be called to testify as a witness in a trial of a friend, or perhaps as agonizing, against someone who you don't know but whose fate is in your hands. and in general, you make things a whole lot easier for the government at a time when we don't notice they're returning the favor.
>
> we, as a people, face four more years. to survive is a necessity. but to flower, we must be alive—and *well*. that's going to take love, strength, togetherness, unity, power, hope—and more love. if some folks ain't felt all that yet, and it's a lot, that don't mean we're not gonna make it. after sorrow comes joy.

Some people (in addition to the Fort Worth Five) appear to have refused to testify as a matter of principle. Two women who were organizers of the May Day demonstrations refused to testify, even after they were granted the maximum "transactional immunity." They escaped their contempt sentence only because the government did not want to disclose the extent of its wiretapping of the May Day operation. Twelve people were subpoenaed to testify as ISD sought to resurrect charges against Leslie Bacon regarding the bombing of the New York bank. All refused to testify and, further, served as plaintiffs in an affirmative legal suit against the grand jury. After Bacon was indicted in connection with the bank attacks, the subpoenas were withdrawn; they have not been reinstituted. These witnesses were lucky—apparently, ISD made a judgment that it was not worth pursuing them or that it could not because of legal impediments. However, the witnesses in Tucson felt the full brunt of the contempt sanction. All five, upon refusing to testify after receiving transactional immunity, were imprisoned under civil contempt. They had to remain in prison until they agreed to testify or until the grand jury expired. The maximum life of a regular grand jury is normally eighteen months, although it can be extended. They remained in jail from November 1970 through March 25, 1971. When they finally secured their release at the expiration of the grand jury, Guy Goodwin subpoenaed them again! Faced with an apparently endless round of jailings, the five finally gave up and began to testify. (One witness, Lee Weinberg, was concerned about the custody of her children if she went to jail.) None of their testimony was self-incriminating, so their resistance over the four months was primarily a protest against governmental power's being exercised simply because it is possessed. One could adopt a rather straightforward, no-nonsense position on the case of these five—they should either talk or bear the consequences. It may, however, appear otherwise if one believes that the grand jury was being used covertly for group intimidation, with the hope that resistance would provide an occasion for jailing people who are simply ideologically and politically committed to protecting their associates from unwarranted governmental intrusion.

# XI.

---

## The Grand Jury:
## Out of Line with
## the Bill of
## Rights

The Bacon, Tucson, and Fort Worth cases further illustrate the potential for attack by a grand jury because it has few of the controls that normally govern the criminal process. I have alluded to the fact that all kinds of evidence that could not be used at a trial are permitted into the grand jury (e.g., hearsay), but the absence of procedural protections is more extensive than that. The constitutional prohibition against double jeopardy bars the government from giving the defendant a second sentence for the same offense. Yet the Tucson group faced jailing a second time for refusal to answer the same questions that they had been asked the first time they were imprisoned. The Fort Worth Five spent approximately 10 months in jail—and had no right to demand a trial by jury.

A defendant facing an ordinary criminal charge, for which he can receive at least 6 months in jail, has an absolute constitutional right to a trial by jury.* Under the *Miranda*** case, the police must tell a suspect whom they arrest and interrogate that he has a right to remain silent, to have a lawyer present during the questioning, and to *stop* talking at any time he desires. He also has a right to have his attorney present and to cross-examine prosecution witnesses during a preliminary hearing.† None of these warnings or legal protections is accorded *any* grand jury witness, not even the prime suspect, should he be called before the grand jury. Once Leslie Bacon began to discuss before the grand jury some of her activities that may have been incriminating, she was required to continue to discuss them, unlike an interrogation in a police station or by a prosecutor lacking a grand jury subpoena.‡ The witness has an obligation to testify before the grand jury to all questions save those to which he makes a specific, timely objection on Fifth Amendment grounds, or on the basis of some other well-established privilege (e.g., husband–wife).

The courts have rationalized the broad grand jury power to inquire by saying that the suspect can at least be summoned, for he might waive any privileges he has not to testify. In this sense, the subpoena is tantamount to that

*Baldwin v. New York* 399 U.S. 66 (1970).

**Miranda v. Arizona* 384 U.S. 486 (1966).

†The preliminary hearing performs roughly the same function as the grand jury in that a determination is made as to whether there is enough evidence to hold a defendant for trial. The difference is that the defendant has a right to be present during the hearing (unlike the grand jury), and the determination to dismiss or require the defendant to go to trial is made by the judge.

‡To their credit, many prosecutors have begun telling people who are suspects that they have a right not to incriminate themselves and a right to consult an attorney.

issued to require a witness to testify at a criminal trial, or roughly analogous to an arrest and the beginning of police interrogation. However, the courts have also said that a witness or suspect must respond to questions to which he cannot invoke the Fifth Amendment because he may be a source of evidence on other offenders. This would also be true in a police station interrogation, but the defendant there has the right to total silence.

The court's rule in the police station context gives more realistic protection to the Fifth Amendment because it may be very difficult for a layman (or even those legally trained) to define precisely which matters may or may not be self-incriminatory; the court's decisions in this area are quite complicated.[1] Therefore, the option of total silence relieves the suspect of making difficult selective responses.

Not only is the witness faced with making legal decisions for which he may be ill equipped, but prosecutors (who, it must be remembered, are not monitored by a judge in the grand jury room) have tried to intimidate witnesses into surrendering their right not to testify by resorting to humiliating, high-pressured interrogation. Professor Samuel Popkin, a specialist on Vietnam from Harvard University, was badgered in this fashion. Called before a Boston grand jury in March 1972, ostensibly because he was acquainted with Daniel Ellsberg (who had been charged with theft and release of the Pentagon Papers), he and the prosecutor engaged in the following coloquy:

Q: Mr. Popkin, more specifically, do you know if someone possessed what is now known as the Pentagon Papers in Massachusetts other than to the extent you have previously testified?
A: May I see my lawyers?
Q: Mr. Popkin, as you know, a witness has the right to see his lawyers only on serious questions. You have been out

of the room twice already for periods as long as ten minutes. You are now asking permission to leave the room for a third time. Is this necessary?

Q: Mr. Popkin, do you recall an immediate reaction that was formed in your mind upon hearing about original stories in *The New York Times* about who may have been the source?

A: I request permission to see my counsel.

Q: Mr. Popkin, how can your counsel be of use in this case? We're asking you about your immediate reaction.

A: I request permission to see my counsel.

Q: Mr. Popkin, you are being asked about your immediate opinion, how can your counsel be relevant?

A: I request permission to see my counsel.

Q: Mr. Popkin, you are stretching things for this grand jury. Your exits from the room have been ranging about five minutes. This is being an inconvenience for the grand jury.

In addition to the pressure on a witness' Fifth Amendment rights, Fourth Amendment rights may also not be respected in the grand jury. A witness may be forced to produce evidence, even though the prosecutor offers no proof that it is linked to criminal activity. He can also be the butt of an unlawful invasion of privacy in which the police have broken into his house without a warrant, and still be made to answer questions on the basis of what the police have seen or taken.

In *Davis v. Mississippi,** the court reversed a conviction in which the prosecution used as evidence fingerprints taken from the defendant when he was among 24 people who were detained for fingerprinting. The court clearly stated that "detentions for the sole purpose of obtaining fingerprints are no less subject to the constraints of the

---

*394 U.S. 721 (1969).

Fourth Amendment,"* and objected to the police's dragnet method of arresting so many people when they had no prior evidence linking any of them, including the defendant, to the crime. In *United States v. Dionisio,*\*\* the court allowed a prosecutor to call 20 people before the grand jury to secure prints of their voices, even though, as in the *Davis* case, the prosecution produced no prior evidence that any of them were connected to criminal activity. These two cases must teach law enforcement officials that police cannot conduct dragnets but that prosecutors can, or, more likely, that when the police want to conduct a dragnet they ought to get the prosecutor to do it for them through the grand jury.

The *Calandra†* case followed on the heels of *Dionisio* and diluted Fourth Amendment rights further. The prosecution asked the witness questions based on material seized illegally, either with no warrant or under a defective warrant. The court held that even though Calandra could have objected to the use of the evidence to interrogate him were he a defendant at trial,‡ he could not object in the grand jury.

How is it that a witness, or even a potential defendant, is deprived of these many constitutional protections in the grand jury proceeding? The answer lies in the unique role the courts have assigned to the grand jury and the *sui generis* nature of the contempt sanction attached to it. In general, a witness is not accorded the legal rights accorded indictees and defendants because he is not, at that point, being charged with a crime. However, even a witness whom the prosecutor seeks to indict does not have the protections

*Davis v. Mississippi* 394 U.S. 721 (1969) p. 727.

\*\*410 U.S. 1 (1973).

†*U.S. v. Calandra,* 94 S. Ct. 613 (1974).

‡*Mapp v. Ohio,* 367 U.S. 643 (1961).

that he must be accorded in interrogation by the prosecutor or the police outside the grand jury. (Claims that a prosecutor should not be able to subpoena a potential defendant have not been sustained.)

The reason counsel is barred from the grand jury room is that the proceedings are "nonadversarial" and the witness is deemed to have the maximum protection that he needs because he can invoke his right not to give testimony that is incriminating. Other consequences flow from the fact that the contempt proceedings are technically denominated "civil" and not "criminal." Thus, a witness does not have a right to a jury trial because no "criminal" offense is deemed to have been committed; rather, the court is using "remedial" measures to deal with the obstruction of its processes by the witness. Under civil contempt, the witness can secure his own release any time he chooses to testify. Since the imprisonment is not for a fixed and definite term, it is not a "criminal" sentence. Thus, a second refusal to testify becomes a new occasion for the application of the "nonpunitive" measure, and the witness is said to have the alternative of avoiding their imposition by testifying.

It is hard to define the full scope of the decisions concerning the Fourth Amendment and the grand jury, but they do emphasize a potential for making the grand jury a special, uncontrolled oasis for the prosecution, undermining constitutional rights that the court has been laboriously developing. The *Dionisio* case may be limited because the court claimed that privacy was not invaded by a subpoena for voice prints, since we regularly exhibit our voices in public. But *Davis* would have limited the taking of fingerprints, even though we regularly leave them in public, to "narrowly defined circumstances"*—which should mean, if the case controls the grand jury, that you cannot bring

*Davis v. Mississippi,* op. cit., p. 727.

masses of people under subpoena to be fingerprinted, but
that you must show some reason for choosing that particular group. For example, if a weapon used in a crime had a
set of fingerprints on it and was found in an apartment, a
prosecutor could probably get a warrant to fingerprint the
five people who he could show regularly frequented that
apartment. The court in *Dionisio,* however, did not use the
qualifying language of *Davis,* and there may be no such requirement that has to be met for the grand jury.*

The *Calandra* case is of more import, and probably
was the opening gambit of the new Nixon appointees' attempt to overrule the *Mapp* case, which excludes illegally
seized evidence from trial. On its face, however, the decision was limited to the grand jury, and again, its unique-
ness was emphasized. It is not, the court said, the place where
ultimate guilt or innocence is determined, and since the
police know that the prosecutor cannot use illegally seized
evidence at trial, there is no *additional* deterrent effect on
the police to bar its use in the grand jury.

Why, then, did the prosecution press so assiduously to
interrogate Calandra? The reason was that if it could not
get evidence against him, it might against others—obviously
true, since Calandra was not the prime target and was given
immunity. The case points up the anomaly of the rules
governing "standing" to object—that is, making a defendant

*For example, can people be subpoenaed, without having been
arrested, to appear in lineups conducted in the grand jury? We
exhibit our faces and bodies publicly, so presumably there is no
"privacy" interest invaded. The Supreme Court has given defendants a right to have counsel present during lineups, but this has
been limited to lineups conducted after an indictment. So the
fact that defense counsel is barred from the grand jury—a preindictment proceeding—would present no problem. But cf. *In
re Schoefield,* 486 F 2d. 85 (1973), which did not read *Dionisio,*
as absolving the prosecutor of making some showing of a basis
for subpoenaing certain information.

at trial prove that *his* constitutional rights were violated before allowing him to object to unconstitutional police behavior. If *any* defendant could object to *any* illegally seized evidence (as is done in California), this would provide the maximum pressure on the police to avoid illegal searches. But the decision is troublesome in two further respects, one of which is especially pertinent to the "new-style" grand juries. First, the *Calandra* case required the court to hold a witness in contempt who refuses to participate in the further exploitation of an invasion of his privacy. The reward for a witness' pointing out and resisting the illegal police behavior, therefore, was jail. Second, the court treated the grand jury as if it were only a vehicle for seeking indictments, probably because the factual context of *Calandra* involved garden variety criminal activity (gambling). The court was, therefore, not compelled to deal with the fact that the grand jury could be (and has been) used for harassment and gathering intelligence on the government's political opposition. If this were the goal of the prosecution, it might very well engage in illegal searches as a device for forcing a witness to make further disclosures about the nature of his political organization and allies.

# XII.

---

## Newsmen and Scholars: Informing the Public or Informing the Police?

The intensified use of the compulsory process of the grand jury has not been limited to antiadministration militants and activists but has also reached people essential to an informed public, namely, scholars writing on important issues and newsmen covering current events on a daily or weekly basis. There has always been some tension between the perceived need of journalists to perform their publishing and communicating function without interference, and the demands of the criminal justice system either for access to all sources of evidence or for keeping jurors from being prejudiced by pretrial publicity. However, subpoenas of the press were so rare until 1969 that there are only 11 recorded instances in which reporters have felt the need to invoke state statutes exempting them from the grand jury process.[1] However, between 1969 and 1972, during the Nixon administration's first term in office, at least 124 subpoenas were served on the National Broadcasting Company and the Columbia Broadcasting System alone, and approximately 25 newmen either went to jail for resisting grand jury subpoenas or were threatened with that possibility.

The reasons for this burgeoning resort to newsman for information appear to be both political and technological. The news media were not caught up in the subpoena process in the past for two reasons: First, newsmen may have been more cooperative in supplying law enforcement officials with information when it was not derived from confidential relationships. Second, when they had not developed the information independently, the sources they relied on were hostile to the people they reported on and, thus, would not oppose their cooperation with the police. (This happened sometimes with the Ku Klux Klan and the Mafia.) However, when it came to the political left, the liberal sector of the press was able to develop articles only on the basis of confidential relationships. But the left became a main target of the Nixon administration and attracted nonstop inquiries of newsmen privy to its activities.

Many newsmen believe that free and unimpeded functioning in their particular line of work is key to preserving the free speech guaranteed by the First Amendment. They feel it absolutely essential that the government respect that amendment's prohibition against "abridging the freedom of speech, or of the press" by forgoing any action that restricts, curtails, or suppresses the free flow of information. Some of these claims may be self-interest masquerading in free speech rhetoric, but most of us would agree that if people are to govern themselves effectively in a democratic society, it must be on an informed basis—and thus, maximum access to information is absolutely essential. Newsmen reason that if they are forced to disclose their sources of confidential information, sources that value anonymity will cease cooperating.

The pressure on the media to disclose their sources has come not only from the Nixon administration and federal grand juries but also from local prosecutors using state grand juries, from litigants in civil matters, and from defendants in criminal trials—all issuing subpoenas in the attempt to get information. Because we are here concerned only with the operation of the grand jury, we will not explore the problems presented by subpoenas to appear before congressional committees or at pretrial or trial stages of civil litigation, or those issued when a defendant seeks a newsman's testimony to aid his defense in a criminal trial. In each such situation the variables that must be taken into account and the interests to be balanced differ from those we must consider when dealing with the grand jury. One could, for example, propose a ban on grand jury subpoenas as a means of protecting newsmen's access to confidential information, and yet support the right of a citizen suing a newspaper for libel to subpoena all the information needed to support the charge. Perhaps the right to protect sources cannot be carried so far as to permit a newspaper to injure the reputation of a person who has no equivalent chance to respond and to simultaneously withhold information that is in its exclusive control and necessary for the subject of their stories to prove he was libeled.

Both the state and federal grand juries have begun to increase their subpoenas to newsmen who possess technological resources to prove or disprove the occurrence of particular events. The unaided memories or perceptions of witnesses are highly subject to error and distortion; hence the search for trained observers, especially those who may have recorded the events in notes, tape recordings, or film.

Given the long delay in bringing on a criminal matter for trial, these more unimpeachable sources of evidence are valued even more. We are concentrating here, however, on instances in which the journalist or writer has been subpoenaed to disclose the source of information because the source either is suspected of a crime or may have evidence that another person committed a crime, or when the reporter himself may be suspected of participating in a crime such as receiving documents alleged to have been stolen.

At the federal level, it is not at all surprising that the gun of grand jury inquiry has been trained on newsmen, above and beyond the need to preserve evidence in a more accurate form. Over the eleven-year span of the Vietnam War, newsmen developed an increasing distrust of governmentally "packaged" explanations for American foreign policy because of the fabrications and half-truths they were fed about U.S. action and motives in that war. The serious questioning of the veracity and reliability of federal officials had reached its height at the time Nixon was elected President. The major blame for journalists' disaffection, thus, cannot be attributed to Nixon; it had gathered its greatest momentum during preceding Democratic administrations, especially that of Lyndon B. Johnson. Nixon did, however, bring a special distrust of the press that may help explain the coercive tactics his administration aimed at the media. Throughout his political career he has seen the press, especially its liberal wing, as conducting a personal vendetta against him. Spiro Agnew, when he was vice president, built a reputation for "outspokenness" based largely on his vigorous attacks, and sometimes veiled threats, against the media. It is difficult to document the extent to which the administration's verbal volley at the press was being orchestrated into more concrete counterattacks, but some evidence from the Senate Watergate Committee hearings indicated that the White House was considering a campaign against its critics, including antitrust suits against those owning more than one news outlet in a given area, special Internal Revenue Service scrutiny of their taxes, and Federal Communications Commission monitoring of radio and TV news broadcasts to establish charges of bias or slanted news.[2]

Thus, not only were militants and activists under attack, but also the media that focused on their activities or appeared to be a conduit for presenting and, worse, interpreting their criticism of the Nixon administration.

The case best illustrating all these elements is Earl Caldwell's, in which the Supreme Court had to decide whether newsmen had a constitutional exemption from the grand jury process. Caldwell, a black reporter for *The New York Times*, covered the 1967 riots and, incidental to that task, developed contacts with the leadership of the Black Panther party.

These contacts were developed slowly and with difficulty because the Panthers were well aware that they were under heavy surveillance, that police intelligence units sometimes have their men pose as journalists, and that real journalists have sometimes cooperated with the police even though they made promises of confidentiality. Further, Caldwell, as a middle-class black working for a white establishment institution, was not likely to draw quick acceptance from a group that places primary reliance on the black "lumpen proletariat" of American urban ghettos to achieve social change. With all of this working against him, however, Caldwell did manage to spend days and nights in the Panthers' offices, taping interviews with some of the leadership. After his stories were published in *The New York Times,* he began to receive frequent visits from FBI agents, asking for information on the Panthers that had not yet appeared in his stories. Caldwell, mindful of the Panthers' initial suspicions that he was "an agent," referred the FBI men to his news stories, saying that there was nothing outside of published stories that he could tell them. When the FBI became frustrated with his failure to cooperate, it told someone in his office, "You just tell Caldwell we're tired of playing with him. If he doesn't want to tell it to us, he'll tell it to the court."[3] Two days later he was called before a San Francisco grand jury.

Caldwell knew that the Panthers were watching the whole drama; indeed, two of the workers on the Panther newspaper were subpoenaed around the same time and queried about the operation of the newspaper and the internal structure of the Panther organization. He also knew that for him even to appear in a secret session of the grand jury, after which they would have only his word that he had given no information damaging to their organization or exploitative of their confidences, would seriously jeopardize his credibility with the group.

Because of the peculiar sensitivity of the Panthers, Caldwell felt that he had to demand the maximum protection and refuse to appear at all, even though the trial judge issued a protective order exempting him from revealing his confidential sources or any information received in the course of news gathering, unless the statements were given to him for publication. Instead, Caldwell chose to risk contempt and jail.

Initially, things turned out well for Caldwell. The court of appeals said that when the news-gathering function might be jeopardized by his mere appearance, the government must demonstrate a "compelling need" for his presence and for his testimony before he could be subpoenaed. This court tried to narrow its ruling by noting that this exemption from appearance before the grand jury was limited to news sources that were as sensitive as the Black

Panther party respecting the appearance of a breach of confidentiality.*

Some, like Samuel Popkin of Harvard University and Noam Chomsky of the Massachusetts Institute of Technology, who write on public issues as scholars and not as newsmen, thought they had no claim to a First Amendment exemption from a grand jury appearance upon being subpoenaed. This is curious in one sense, because they are among that new breed termed the "public scholar," who may need *more* protection than the average journalist with a daily newspaper.** As social and political change has accelerated and public issues have become more complex, the journalist under pressure to publish a new story each day may be unable to keep the public fully informed on controversial issues. Into this void have stepped the "public scholars"—researchers and academicians doing in-depth investigative fact-finding that permits a subject to be thoroughly analyzed in all of its complexity. Because of the seriousness of their work and because they primarily observe and comment on the operations of government, they ought to be freer to publish so as to provide the public with an adequate assessment and criticism of the performance of government officials.

For example, all of the scholars who were subpoenaed, Popkin, Chomsky, and Richard Falk of Princeton Uni-

*The "sensitivity" of the Panthers is not a function of paranoia—the FBI has been forced to admit that it engaged in a counter-intelligence program against them to prevent them from coalescing with other black nationalist groups, from developing a charismatic leader, and from gaining respectability. *The New York Times*, March 8, 1974, p. 15, col. 1.

**Congress has given some minimal recognition to the distinction by protecting drug researchers. See Chapter XVII, footnote, on page 129.

versity, were heavily involved in research and writing about the Vietnam War, making strong criticisms of governmental policy that were sorely needed by the public.* However, given the fact that their confidential sources are primarily people in high places in the government, they apparently did not feel that they had to take their objection as far as refusing to appear before the grand jury. The prime concern of their sources would be the maintenance of anonymity; after the scholars appeared before the grand jury, the sources would know that the assurances of confidentiality had been respected if they were not subjected to dismissal, demotion, or other reprisals.

The problem for scholars is best illustrated by the course of events for Samuel Popkin. He attended the grand jury sessions but refused to answer questions that would have required disclosure of his sources for research on Vietnam and the Pentagon Papers. The court of appeals upheld Popkin's refusal, but only to the extent that the questioning required the disclosure of confidential sources who were either government officials or other partcipants in the disclosure of the Pentagon Papers. This meant, however, that Popkin would have to disclose the names of *other* scholars with whom he had worked, and who might have told him which government officials *they* had worked with. When Popkin took the position that such a limitation would betray his confidential sources, he became the first American scholar to be jailed for protecting his sources of information.

Popkin's case, however, is illustrative of the milder treatment that the Justice Department accorded newsmen and scholars who were visible and supported by influential institutions. The Harvard faculty had adopted a resolution that publicly urged governmental restraint on probes into

*The court threw out subpoenas directed at Falk and Chomsky because the Justice Department refused to make an unequivocal denial that they had been subjected to illegal wiretapping.

scholarly research. Derek Bok, president of Harvard University and a lawyer, joined the case to argue in Popkin's favor; and Daniel Steiner, general counsel for that university, met privately with A. William Olson, then head of the Internal Security Division, to urge Popkin's early release. The government suddenly decided to dismiss the grand jury, and thus Popkin spent only one week in prison.* The less coercive treatment of newsmen may reflect government's fear of the publicity generated when a newsman is jailed, but it may also mean that the newsmen and scholars were not key to the development of information. It was the *Caldwell* victory at the court of appeals, however, that gave Popkin and others an incentive to resist subpoenas and to assert their First Amendment rights. For the first time, a federal court carved out a zone of freedom in which reporters could operate with confidential sources. Some newsmen began telling their confidential sources that the *Caldwell* case gave them more protection than the personal word of the reporter.

While lower federal courts began to follow the *Caldwell* case, state court judges were regularly holding reporters in contempt. Two such cases involved Paul M. Branzburg of the Louisville *Courier-Journal* and Paul Pappas of WTEZ-TV in New Bedford, Massachusetts, and were ultimately decided by the Supreme Court at the same time as *Caldwell*. Branzburg was subpoenaed after he ran articles about a local plant where he had observed marijuana being

*Truman Capote served only a few days in jail for refusing to disclose the nature of confidential interviews with prisoners, and an editor of the student newspaper at the University of Oregon was only fined ($300) when she refused to testify about a story on student use of marijuana. "Press Subpoenas: Privilege in a Time of Violence," Vince Blasi, *The Nation*, December 21, 1970, p. 654. Earl Caldwell was never recalled before the grand jury, even after losing his case.

treated and packaged for sale. There was a state "shield" law exempting newsmen from having to disclose their sources, but the state court took an end run on the statute and said that it did not apply if the newsmen had "observed" the source committing a crime. The Supreme Court, thus, was presented with a more modest proposition in the *Branzburg* case than in *Caldwell,* namely, that reporters do not have to disclose the identity of the source of any story that they publish. If the court was bothered by the fact that the reporter had witnessed the commission of an offence, it might have limited its exemption to those observations, which would not have been permitted without the assurance of confidentiality. Thus, if a reporter, like any other citizen, saw a crime committed, *independent* of any assurance of confidentiality, then he would have to testify.

If the Court, however, was bothered by the exemption of a reporter who had actually observed the commission of a crime, even a nonviolent crime as in *Branzburg,* it was certainly presented a third choice for fashioning some protection for newsmen in the *Pappas* case. During the summer of 1970 the Black Panthers were expecting a particularly rough police raid on their headquarters, and they asked newsman Pappas to spend the night and record the officers' methods of entry and search. There was, in fact, no raid, and the agreement that Pappas had with the Panthers was that unless the raid occurred he would make no disclosures about his stay in their headquarters. The Court was, thus, not necessarily dealing with a reporter who had witnessed a crime, and could have exempted Pappas from having to testify about the noncriminal activities that he had observed.

The Supreme Court, however, when it decided the *Caldwell, Branzburg,* and *Pappas* cases, took none of these options. The Court said flatly that news gathering gave reporters no constitutional immunity from appearing and testifying before the grand jury.

The Court did say that when a newsman could demonstrate that he was being subpoenaed *solely* to interfere with his news-reporting activities, and not for an investigation of a crime, the courts were authorized to step in and prevent such a grand jury inquiry. This qualification, however, has little practical meaning, because a person subpoenaed before the grand jury has no right to know the nature or scope of the investigation, and the courts credit rather automatically any assertion by the government that there is a legitimate purpose to the inquiry.

The cases were decided by the closest possible judicial margin, 5 to 4. The dissenting judges criticized the "crabbed view of the First Amendment," which they said reflected "a disturbing insensitivity to the critical role of an independent press."* Three of the dissenting judges would have established the same test that the court of appeals adopted in the *Caldwell* case. Justice Douglas went further, saying that the First Amendment protection of free communication was not to be "balanced" against some supposed contrary needs of the government. He thought newsmen had an absolute privilege not to appear before the grand jury. Douglas's position was responsive to one charge made by the majority, which claimed that the proposal by other dissenting judges that the government's need for information be balanced against the need to protect the public's right to know created such a vague standard that a confidential informant might still be deterred from cooperating with newsmen because he could never predict how a court would subsequently strike the balance. Douglas's position, at least, has none of this uncertainty.

While the majority opinion clearly will not facilitate information reaching the public, especially on controversial matters or when government employees wish to complain about secret, but calamitous, policies in their department,

---

*Branzburg v. Hayes,* 408 U.S. 665, 725 (1972).

defining the scope of a newsman's privilege may be more appropriate for a legislature than the court, if only because of the number of variables that must be taken into account and the refined distinctions that must be made.

For example, had the Supreme Court decided that there was a constitutional newsman's privilege, it (or lower courts) would have had to answer the question, Who can claim to be a newsman? Is it only those who work for established, well-known publications, and who make their living through such work? What about a person regularly employed as a lawyer who occasionally writes for a magazine? What about people who write on a gratis and volunteer basis, or only sporadically? These are probably the kinds of questions that are better settled, carefully and with some precision, at the legislative level.

Also, the Court had before it some empirical data developed by Vincent Blasi of the University of Michigan, who thought that any constitutional rule that the Court might adopt should be contoured to the real needs of reporters. His research examined the extent to which newsmen relied on confidential sources and what their estimates were of their continued ability to rely on these sources if confidentially could not be assured.[4] His data, however, would not have convinced the skeptic that all reporters need an absolute, or even qualified, protection of their confidential sources in order to carry out their regular reporting. Only slightly more than half of the reporters said that they relied on confidential sources for even 10 percent of their stories. Only 8 percent were able to say that their professional functioning had, in the past, been hindered by their sources' knowledge that they were subject to subpoena. The reliance on confidential sources increased when the reporter worked for a daily rather than a weekly publication. Younger reporters tended to rely less on confidential sources that their older colleagues, and tended to

see this independence as better reportorial functioning because they avoided the trap of being, in effect, a public re-
lations arm for government officials issuing self-serving
propaganda through "off-the-record" conferences.

Blasi's findings, thus, showed that only special reporters relied, in any critical way, on confidential sources and
that there was no simple, straight-line explanation for the
"drying up" of sources. However, the Supreme Court often
decides constitutional questions without fully developed
data, especially when the data concern complicated human
relationships that can never be completely and definitively
described. The Court has also fashioned rules that have a
speculative impact on only a few people. Under either circumstance, the Court simply takes the best information it
has and does the thing it is uniquely structured to do: adopt
a value framework and then fashion the rules appropriate
to it. The Court was, thus, not barred by Blasi's findings
from opting for protection of the newsman–informer relationship, even if it was crucial only to a few reporters doing
highly sensitive reporting. However, Blasi's data may indicate that the best approach is a legislative one.

In the absence of federal legislation on a newsman's
privilege, responsible law enforcement officials could have
exercised their judgment on a case-by-case basis to subpoena
newsmen only under extreme circumstances; however, the
experience during the Nixon administration would not
make one sanguine about sole reliance on such unfettered
discretion. John Mitchell, while attorney general, apparently was not apprised of the Caldwell subpoena, although
it eventuated in a clash with a major newspaper. It was
issued after the FBI persuaded a local U.S. attorney to do
so. (Congress has refused, on a number of occasions, to grant
power to the FBI to compel people to respond to its inter-
rogations, but the FBI has circumvented this absence of
statutory authority by getting U.S. attorneys to subpoena

people to answer the questions the FBI has previously put
to them.) Mitchell tried to get word to local U.S. attorneys
to subpoena newsmen only as a last resort, and then only
after negotiation. The instruction was not completely
heeded, for CBS was subpoenaed with little effort at negotiation. Mitchell formalized his instructions in guidelines
in August 1970, but in subsequent cases in which newsmen
were able to show that the guidelines had been ignored, the
court (after argument in this vein by U.S. attorneys) held
that the guidelines were only advisory interdepartmental
procedures and did not create any enforceable "rights" in
court.[5]

In his brief stay as attorney general, Elliot Richardson
moved the cautionary guidelines respecting newsmen up
to the status of a departmental order and thus strengthened
the claim that these are mandaιory procedures.[6] His rules,
like Mitchell's, require the personal approval of the attorney general before a newsman is subpoenaed. In addition, such personal approval is required before a member
of the news media is arrested, indicted, or questioned about
any offense that he is suspected of having committed in the
course of covering a news story.

However, during and after Richardson's tenure in office, federal subpoenas to newsmen greatly abated, so no
test has been made of the "mandatory" nature of the new
rules. In any event, the guidelines or regulations may be inadequate, since they only urge that, as a preliminary matter,
some need for the information must be demonstrated and
some effort must be made to get "cooperation." Newsmen
are, thus, not given any qualified or absolute privilege not
to be coerced to testify. Consequently, legislation may be
the only route to greater definiteness where protection is
warranted.

The Department of Justice has objected to federal legislation on the ground that newsmen are adequately pro-

tected by its own internal regulation.[7] The Department claims that it has denied 7 requests from local U.S. attorneys for issuance of subpoenas against newsmen because of non-compliance with its own internal guidelines. Further, it claims that only 17 subpoenas have been issued since the August 1970 guidelines. Two of these subpoenas involved inquiry about confidential sources, but the subpoenas were issued at the request of the reporters after an agreement by the newsmen to "cooperate." It is difficult to accept the notion that none of these newsmen felt compromised in their professional functioning and that their "cooperation" was completely voluntary, for there were few cases clearly supporting the right of newsmen to resist a subpoena during those years, and certainly after the 1972 *Caldwell* decision reporters knew that federal officials did not need their "agreement" to get whatever information they wanted. The Department also reports that "sometimes" newsmen provided information without requesting the formality of the issuance of a subpoena. We are not told how many such instances there were or how often they involved probing confidential sources. These "voluntary" profferings may also have been a product of the newsmen's knowledge that coercive measures were readily available to federal officials who questioned them. The Justice Department provided no assessment of the material subpoenaed or of the resultant indictments and convictions so that one could gauge whether they were following their own standard of seeking only information that was "essential." In toto, if we recognize some serious free speech interests as being involved, it is unwise to leave untrammeled discretion in law enforcement officials, for they are apt to regard their efficiency in apprehending and prosecuting offenders as far more important than the more nebulous goal of protecting the public's access to information.

# XIII.

---

# The Public Official and the Grand Jury— Congress Versus the Executive Branch

The encounter that public officials have had with the grand jury has had a muzzling effect similar to that for newsmen and scholars. The case of Senator Mike Gravel has raised many issues concerning the public's right to know, but it has profound political implications because the legislative branch of government, theoretically coequal to the judiciary, has had its processes curtailed and subordinated in the interest of allowing the grand jury the broadest scope for inquiry.

In June 1971, Senator Gravel convened a meeting of the Subcommittee on Buildings and Grounds of the Public Works Committee, read portions of the Pentagon Papers, and thereafter placed the entire 47 volumes in the public record. Leonard Rodberg, an aide of the senator and a fellow at the Institute of Policy Studies, assisted the senator in preparing and conducting the hearing. Senator Gravel had also contacted Howard Webber, an editor at M.I.T. Press, about publishing the Pentagon Papers. The alleged "theft" of this history of the Vietnam War, which had been classified as "secret" and thus withheld from the public, was then under a grand jury investigation. Rodberg and Webber were subpoenaed after it became known that Senator Gravel had made the Pentagon Papers a matter of public record in his subcommittee deliberations. They resisted the subpoena on the grounds that a senator is constitutionally protected against inquiry about his legislative duties—thus, they must also be immune because they were only assisting him in the performance of those duties.

The newsmen's claim of a First Amendment privilege was not strong, probably because the precedents derived from English law, which illuminate many of our constitutional provisions, gave little support to the claim. Further, outside of the broad wording of the First Amendment, there was no specific constitutional provision that identified such a privilege and the people it covered. By contrast, the claim of Senator Gravel and his aides was clearly on stronger grounds. A specific provision of the federal Constitution directly protects the freedom of speech of members of Congress by stating that "for any Speech or Debate in either House, they shall not be questioned in any other Place."[1] Also, there is less difficulty in identifying the people to whom this privilege extends than would be the case with newsmen. The same five judges who decided the *Caldwell* case, constituting the majority in this case as well, stated that the senator and his aides were immune from grand jury questioning under the constitutional provision only regarding activities strictly pertinent to carrying out the subcommittee's functions.* This did not include arranging for sub-

---

*Gravel v. United States,* 408 U.S. 606 (1972).

sequent publication in the general press; thus those activities were subject to grand jury inquiry. Insofar as possession of the documents may have been a criminal offense, the Court would also have permitted inquiry into how the senator or his aides obtained the Pentagon Papers.

That possibility directly raised the question presented in the newsmen's case, namely, whether members of Congress who receive material that aids their legislative function will not be blocked from effectively using it if the executive branch, which controls the grand jury process, can force disclosures of names of people who have leaked information that criticizes that branch's functioning. In one sense, the ruling seriously limits the extent to which the public will be kept fully informed, especially about governmental affairs. The role of the press and the media as vigorous critics of government has hardly been sterling. The media have been cowed from covering major antiwar demonstrations, and one TV station has been discouraged from providing immediate analysis of Presidential speeches. This is due partially to the fact that private stations must look to the executive branch for the renewal of their licenses, and public television, for funding. Even the press, exempt from these controls, lagged in its exposure of the full scope of administration involvement in Watergate, though the break-in occurred some five months before the 1972 election. The full exposure was primarily the work of one newspaper, the Washington *Post,* which continued to dog the story.

Therefore, any court decision that weakens the capacity for additional independent criticism by one branch of government of another is serious. One could have expected members of Congress to court publicity by performing a watchdog role over the excesses and abuses in the executive branch, simply because it would foster their reelection. The same judicial decision also has serious implications for the

continued viability of the separation of powers among the
three branches of government. Congress itself has relin-
quished some of its functions to the executive (e.g., war-
making), and now the judiciary has given a narrow defini-
tion of the scope of its legislative power. Sealing the executive off from criticism by confidential informants within
that branch is particularly unfortunate, since such information aids Congress in recouping some of its lost powers. We
have seen the importance of Congress' reassuming control
when it brought rein on an executive who was conducting
a war secretly, unilaterally, and with purposes unrevealable
to the public. The *Gravel* decision has the unfortunate potential of deterring Congress from this new promise of
assertion.

The dissenting judges feared as much. They quarreled
strenuously with the majority position that informing the
public of actions and deliberations undertaken in Congress
was not a natural, indeed essential, part of the legislative
function. They therefore argued for immunizing any pub-
lishers of information already made a matter of public
record, as in the Gravel disclosure, from being questioned
in any manner about that publication on the ground that
they were performing a function that the federal legislator
has a duty to perform, that is, keeping constituents informed of his actions.

The decision had a serious import because of a special
factor Justice Douglas stressed in dissenting: The executive,
under the catchall of "national security," may have already
developed a substantial capacity for burying its own dead
bodies. He points out that 30,000 people in the executive
branch are authorized to keep a document from view by
classifying it "secret," and that the State and Defense De-
partments and the Atomic Energy Commission have over
20 million such documents. Furthermore, Congress appro-
priates approximately $15 billion a year for military and

defense purposes, and the claim of secrecy prevents most of them from knowing how the money is used. Consequently, when someone is brave enough to break through this morass of self-perpetuating and self-protecting classification systems, Douglas would permit the grand jury to call the reporter he has dealt with only if the material bore directly on some "future, sensitive planning of the government."* This limitation, he noted, did not characterize the Pentagon Papers.

*Gravel v. United States, op. cit., p. 642.

# XIV.

---

The Public
Official and the
Grand Jury:
Punishment by
Publicity

The previous discussion of newsmen, scholars, and congressmen was premised on the notion that maximum public exposure of critical issues is healthy for a democratic society and that the countervailing intelligence or investigation needs of the state should be subordinated to that end as much as possible. However, what is the appropriate accommodation of conflicting constitutional claims when the exposure of a public issue occurs through illegal leaks from a grand jury investigation? And what is the proper balance when such leaks jeopardize the rights of a person who may be indicted to be free from the pretrial publicity that prejudices the holding of a fair, unbiased trial?

This problem of public exposure of preindictment investigative material is peculiarly a problem for elected officials, who are highly visible. A story about an unknown under investigation (unless he or she is a member of a *group* that has some notoriety) will hardly see the light of day. Such information on a public official, however, will be considered "news," get printed, and receive wide circulation and public attention.

Before his resignation, Vice President Spiro T. Agnew strenuously asserted that his presumption of innocence was diminished by a barrage of leaks from prosecutors close to the grand jury investigating charges that he was involved in tax fraud and conspiracy to commit bribery and extortion. Well before any judicial resolution of these charges, the newspapers and the weeklies began printing both detailed information on the nature of Agnew's alleged criminal acts, and comments attributed to Justice Department attorneys allegedly evaluating the quality of the evidence against him. The Knight newspapers said that Agnew had received pay-offs of $1,000 a week when he was in office in Baltimore, Maryland, and $50,000 in a lump sum payment after he assumed the vice presidency. *Newsweek* reported the names of Agnew's associates in crime and asserted that they had warned Agnew that if he did not use his influence to stop the investigation they would be forced to involve him.[1] The Washington *Post* headlined a report that Agnew's lawyers were plea bargaining,[2] and finally, a report on CBS quoted Assistant Attorney General Henry Peterson as saying, "We've got the evidence. We've got it cold."[3]

Comments or predictions by law enforcement officials for publication on the likelihood of indictment or conviction of a particular suspect are improper, especially if they could encourage prejudgment of the case by people who may later become jurors. This is precisely the charge that the New Left made against J. Edgar Hoover with respect to his public announcements that there was evidence of a conspiracy to kidnap Henry Kissinger before the matter had even been taken before a grand jury. The proper role of law enforcement officials is to gather the evidence, present it to a grand jury, and generally avoid extraneous extrajudicial comment on any pending criminal proceeding.

People who have official duties, including grand jurors, are prohibited under federal law from disclosing any information received during a grand jury investigation. Secrecy at this stage of the proceeding is regarded as having a number of purposes. First, it is supposed to prevent the flight of the person under investigation. Second, if a suspect is not tipped off that an investigation is under way, he will have no occasion to pressure adverse witnesses to perjure themselves or try to reach grand jurors to pressure them not to indict. (The witness, if he is discovered by the defendant later, could be pressured to perjure himself at trial, but the witness would then do so at the risk of perjury charges' being easily proved against him because of his prior inconsistent statements.) Finally, secrecy protects innocent people in the event that no indictment is returned.

The hard question is this: What is the responsibility of the press to adopt restraint when a suspect may be indicted and tried in the community where the stories are published? And, more pertinent, how should the press rein itself in when the leak of the grand jury proceedings has been illegal? Should the reporters be required to disclose the sources of their stories in an investigation of this illegality? Such was precisely the posture that the Agnew affair had assumed, when Judge Walter Hoffman, who presided over the Agnew grand jury, took the unprecedented step of granting Agnew's attorneys the right to subpoena the newsmen who had printed information obtained from grand jury proceedings or their attendant investigations.

Perhaps some of the information given to the grand jury got to newsmen in a manner not directly prohibited by the statutes that control secrecy in the grand jury. A witness before the grand jury is not one of the people legally barred from discussing what took place when he appeared. The witness has this option so that he can talk with his attorney or other people necessary to assist him in the development of his testimony. Some of the information on the Agnew grand jury may have come from people who had been called before it as witnesses. This explanation does not, however, fully resolve the question of whether newspeople have some responsibility or constitutional duty to avoid prejudicing a suspect's forthcoming trial, even if the information is received via the lawful route of witnesses. But when the person who has been the source of the news story is not a witness but, say, one of the grand jurors, we are still presented with the question of whether newsmen should be forced to disclose such sources, as a deterrent to people's breaching the rule of secrecy in the grand jury.

While in hindsight it appears that many of the press stories concerning Agnew were, in the main, true, is "truth" an argument for putting no restraints on the press in such matters and simply letting reporters be as vigorous and probing as they choose? This writer believes that the particular facts of the Agnew case present the strongest argument for some self-restraint by the press, and for some deterrent on exploiting grand jury leaks, in order to protect the defendant's right to a fair trial. Agnew had been steadily attacking newspapers and the media that ultimately leaked items about the grand jury investigation of him. Despite claims by these newspapers that they were simply reporting the "facts," it is hard to believe that many who had been the butts of stinging attacks by Agnew could have helped but be elated by the opportunity to turn the tables.

At least one publication, which specializes in the doings of the news media world, has tried to justify the aggressive preindictment, pretrial reporting that the media engaged in on the grounds that the Agnew counterattack on the press was an attempt to divert the country from the

merits of the charges against him and, indeed, that many of
the leaks that had been attributed to Justice Department
officials may have come from Agnew's attorneys themselves
as a way of manufacturing pretrial publicity, which they
could then claim as a bar to the prosecution of their client.
They point to the fact that the letter from U.S. Attorney
George Beall in Maryland informing attorney Judah Best
that his client, Agnew, was under investigation was deliv-
ered on August 1, 1972. On August 5, one day before Justice
Department officials in Washington, D.C., received a copy
of the letter for the first time, Jerry Landauer of the *Wall
Street Journal* contacted Beall in Baltimore to seek con-
firmation of its contents. On August 7, the Landauer story
appeared; it was the first newspaper account that there was
an investigation of Agnew under way. The clincher, they
say, is that Landauer was not among the nine reporters
subpoenaed by Agnew's attorneys when they were authorized by Judge Hoffman to interrogate media people, and
that Landauer was omitted because they themselves were
the source of his original leak.

There has been no hard evidence that Agnew's attorneys were indeed trying to manipulate pretrial publicity,
and the sequence of events just recited permits only weak
speculation at best. Further, Agnew's attorneys have excellent reputations as to both character and skill. However,
it is precisely the charge that these attorneys were the source
of the leaks and were trying to contrive a phony diversion-
ary defense for their client that argues in favor of requiring
reporters to disclose their sources in this instance. If Agnew
was trying to send up a smoke screen of prejudicial pretrial
publicity, then that attempt should be exposed. Conversely,
if government attorneys were leaking the material in order
to prejudice his right to fair trial, they, too, should be exposed. Here, either the defendant or the public may lose,
but the only way to fix responsibility and provide some

deterrence to improper actions by either defense or government attorneys is to force the reporter to disclose his or her sources.

Buttressing this position is the fact that there is no complete sacrifice of the public's right to know the facts—the only alteration is the *time* at which it learns the full picture. The news media would have had ample opportunity, perhaps during the trial (because the court can protect the defendant by sequestering the jury) or at the conclusion of the trial, to let the public know the full scope of the public corruption involved. Indeed, the facts would have more integrity than the "tips" and off-the-cuff remarks relied on by the press because they would have been developed after full investigation and after being tested in the adversary process of trial. With regard to Agnew, there was no urgent need for the public to receive the information the press was reporting. The urgency was probably due to the rush to "scoop" other newspapers. A defendant's rights should not be sacrificed to the drive of one publication to sell more newspapers than another, especially when his alternative remedies may be nonexistent legally or practically impossible to invoke (I have in mind the rarely granted remedy of injunction), or inadequate (for money damages cannot restore an injured reputation or compensate for improperly encouraging conviction). The threat of required disclosure of sources (or contempt for failure to reveal them) seems to be the only effective deterrent.

Another unfair consequence is the certain jeopardy to a public's officials future election chances. This is especially true when despite newspaper rumors to the contrary, he is not subsequently indicted. It may be speculated that the candidate used "connections" to squelch the prosecution. Agnew's aides said, after the news stories broke about the alleged graft taking, that his chances for future office were absolutely nil, no matter what the subsequent outcome. Similar damage occurred to Mario Biaggi, a New York congressman who was the front-runner in the Democratic primary for mayor of New York City until *The New York Times* published a story claiming that he had taken the Fifth Amendment with respect to thirty questions by the grand jury concerning his personal financial affairs. Biaggi ran a poor third in a field of four candidates, even though the investigation to which he was subpoenaed had not resulted in an indictment against him.

The problem here is akin to the complaint that civil libertarians make about the use of arrest records to deny a person some benefit or opportunity, even though no subsequent conviction was obtained either because charges were dropped or because the defendant was acquitted. The arrest, like a grand jury investigation that focuses on a particular person, is, in a rough sense, no more than a statement that some law enforcement person suspects the person who is taken into custody for questioning. When these preliminary contacts with a citizen are not subsequently validated by conviction, they should not be used collaterally to penalize him. It would be ideal if everyone treated mere arrest or interrogation of a citizen as having little or no evaluative information, but voters who choose candidates on the basis of fragmented information and impressions are hardly likely to ignore a hint that a candidate is involved in criminal wrongdoing.

Suppose, however, that one isolates this factor of "official suspicion" indicated by arrests and grand jury investigations. If an elected official were not indicted, as in the Biaggi case, would the adverse, and probably unfair, publicity be a sufficient basis for requiring a reporter who leaked the candidate's involvement in a grand jury investigation to disclose his source? Probably not. Here, it seems best to rely on the official custodians of the grand jury material to preserve its secrecy, and to take punitive action directly against those who fail this trust, without using the reporter to uncover them as part of the investigation. The interest of the injured party is not as palpable as that of a defendant who faces a criminal trial. Most candidates will be granted a forum to deny the implications of the leak. If the candidate is running for office, he probably has developed some skill in defending himself in public. Biaggi, for example, may have lost ground not so much because of the original newspaper stories about his grand jury appearances as much as from the final impression that he had lied about the content of his grand jury testimony. (Biaggi appeared trapped by the simplistic "law and order" assumptions that he had previously sought to foster in his own constituency, one variation of that philosophy being that taking the Fifth Amendment is an act reserved for "crooks and commies." Thus, he panicked when he found himself wearing that uncomfortable shoe.)

Rumor had it that the news leak about Agnew's investigation came from the local U.S. attorney's office in Baltimore, with the aim of preventing the case from being politically squelched by a White House already besieged by the scandal of a Watergate. However, the very fact that the White House was in the spotlight for its own corrupt practices makes it unlikely that it would have risked another cover-up, especially if an independent local U.S. attorney made clear his determination to carry the prosecution forward. Moreover, a U.S. attorney who believes his case is being hushed up for illegitimate political reasons has the option of making that belief public, and certainly could, like Elliot Richardson, respectably couple it with a resignation. It is unwarranted, however, to prematurely use the media as insurance against having to expose a cover-up later on; such exposure could seriously compromise the defendant's chance to get a fair, unbiased trial.

Newspapers should exercise self-restraint and not publish grand jury testimony that has been disclosed to them in violation of the law, and when self-restraint is absent such publication ought to be discouraged by sanctions. However, what should be the disposition when the grand jury itself seeks to release a report of its activities containing not indictments but, rather, material adverse to defendants already indicted and facing criminal trial? Does the current statutory law permit that practice—and if it does, are those defendants thus deprived of their constitutional right to a fair trial?

Such was the problem presented to Judge John J. Sirica: As the grand jury was handing up indictments against some of the former officials of the Nixon administration in the Watergate matter, it also included a report that it wanted transmitted to the House Judiciary Committee, which was gathering evidence to make a recommendation to the full House as to whether there were sufficient grounds for consideration of a vote of impeachment of the President. The report contained matters concerning the President that the grand jury thought were pertinent to the inquiry by the House committee. Defendants who had been indicted, however, claimed that, to the extent that *they* were mentioned in the report and that it was made public through the impeachment process, they would be exposed to prejudicial and unconstitutional publicity before their trials.

Judge Sirica was, thus, presented with a problem of considerable magnitude, for previous cases dealing with the authority of a federal grand jury to issue reports as well as indictments were in direct conflict. Assuming that a federal grand jury had authority to issue a report, there was no previous case authorizing a report to be sent to Congress for an impeachment proceeding. The guise in which the issue had usually arisen in the past was when a grand jury, believing it had insufficient evidence to indict a particular defendant, still wished to make some public and critical comment on the person or the operation he was involved in. A similar dilemma occurs when a person is named as a co-conspirator and yet is not indicted. In both instances the charge is made that the grand jury is officially accusing people of wrongdoing but simultaneously depriving them of a *judicial* forum in which to respond.

While early state grand juries assumed that they had the power to issue critical reports in addition to handing down indictments, there was much contemporary precedent that, in the absence of an explicit statutory provision authorizing the issuance of reports, the grand jury cannot do so.[4]

The situation in federal courts was confused further by rules of procedure that appeared to restrict the release of grand jury material, when no indictment had resulted, to occasions "preliminary to, or in connection with, a judicial proceeding."[5] The impeachment process, while having some of the quality of a trial, was decidedly not, in any strict sense, a "judicial proceeding."

Sirica decided to release the report to the House committee, and on the defendants' emergency appeal the appellate court said Sirica had done the right thing. Sirica noted that the issuing of reports had a long history with respect to grand juries, and that the limitations of disclosures to "a judicial proceeding" could not have intended frustration of the discharge of a major constitutional function such as congressional impeachment. Sirica noted, also, that the report in question concerned primarily the President and that the defendants were mentioned only incidentally. The appellate court took note of the fact that the President himself made no objection to the transmission of the report.

(It was speculated that this was a tactical move on the part of ex-President Nixon to avoid creating a further impression that he was trying to suppress evidence, but with the awareness not only that the indicted defendants would definitely raise the issue but also that they had the best chance, if there were any chance at all, of blocking the transmission of the report.)

Sirica's judgment was sound. It is not conceivable that any technical rules of procedure or lesser goals, such as protecting the secrecy of the grand jury proceeding, should operate to bar pertinent evidence from a Congress contemplating impeachment—one of the most serious decisions within our constitutional framework. However, the right of the House committee to receive the grand jury report may not fully answer the question of whether the fairness of an indicted defendant's trial has been compromised. In the spirit of fairness, the House committee ought to delete the indicted defendants' names from any public release of the grand jury report, unless such deletion would make the report unintelligible or useless. Since the indicted defendants are not the focus of the impeachment proceedings, the impact of those proceedings on their trial ought to be minimized; if such limitations are not possible, the defendants have a valid claim that the public issuance of a report naming them unduly compromises their right to a fair trial.

# XV.

---

# Abolish the Grand Jury?

If the history of the grand jury reveals an institution that all too often has failed to achieve its idealized function of buffering innocents from official misuse of the power to prosecute, and if, worse still, it has become perverted into a weapon for harassing and silencing the not-so-loyal opposition, questions about its possible abolition squarely confront us. Despite all its hallowed history, England, the country of its birth, abolished it, except for rare cases, in 1933.[1] Many American states have followed suit, and a survey done in 1964 shows that only five states require prosecution of *all* crimes by indictment, serious or not, and 22 require it only for the serious offences; in 23 others, prosecution by "information" or the initiation of the criminal charges on the complaint of the prosecution alone is an alternative to the grand jury process.[2] Use of this alternative was facilitated by a Supreme Court decision some 90 years ago that found that the grand jury was not so fundamental to criminal justice as to be a mandatory way of beginning prosecutions.[*] During that span of time the Court had sometimes held that

---

[*]*Hurtado v. California,* 110 U.S. 516 (1884).

certain provisions of the Bill of Rights that explicitly controlled the federal government in criminal prosecutions did not apply to the states. While it has subsequently reversed that position and now requires state defendants to have the same protection as federal defendants, it has not done so with respect to the requiring of a grand jury.* It is, obviously, not viewed as indispensable to a fair prosecution.

Abolition of the grand jury would eliminate some present financial costs: payment of grand jurors, witnesses, and personnel who administer the system. It would obviate the loss of income to grand jurors receiving less for sitting than the pay from their regular employment. Since one study indicates that grand jurors refuse to indict in only 3 percent of the cases brought before them, the thin line of protection accorded people against whom there is insufficient evidence may not be worth the expense. This is especially true since, under the less expensive alternatives of having the prosecutor in sole control, innocent people may get the same protection from responsible prosecutors who would not press a weak case to trial. In a fair percentage of the instances after which the grand jury refuses to indict, even the prosecutor agrees that the evidence was insufficient.

---

*Gideon v. Wainwright* 372 U.S. 335 (1963) overruling *Betts v. Brady* 316 U.S. 455 (1942) (6th Amendment right to appointed defense counsel); *Mapp v. Ohio* 367 U.S. 643 (1961) overruling *Wolf v. Colorado* 338 U.S. 25 (1949) (4th Amendment excludes illegally seized evidence from trial); *Malloy v. Hogan* 378 U.S. 1 (1964) overruling *Twining v. New Jersey* 211 U.S. 78 (1908) (Fifth Amendment privilege against self-incrimination); *Duncan v. Louisiana* 391 U.S. 145 (1968) overruling *Maxwell v. Dow* 176 U.S. 581 (1900) (Sixth Amendment right to jury trial); *Benton v. Maryland* 395 U.S. 784 (1969) overruling *Palko v. Connecticut* 302 U.S. 319 (1937) (5th Amendment prohibition against Double Jeopardy); *Pointer v. Texas* 380 U.S. 400 (1965) overruling *West v. Louisiana* 194 U.S. 258 (1903) 6th Amendment right of defendant to cross-examine witnesses against him).

In some instances prosecutors are able to gather all the evidence they need to prosecute without use of the subpoena power of the grand jury. Abolition of the grand jury would reduce the drain on the time of law enforcement and prosecuting personnel in these cases, in which they have to go through the motions of presenting the case to a grand jury to get its formal approval. This is especially true when the prosecutor has overwhelming evidence of guilt.

The only loss to the prosecution through abolition of the grand jury would be the subpoena power, but abolition would present us with the clean and uncluttered question of whether we want prosecutors to have that power. Prosecutors now exercise the power through the grand jury, which is theoretically an arm of the court and not a tool of the executive, and they apparently have used it to gather information without an immediate indictment as the goal. Indeed, we would be required to ask a question we now avoid: Do we wish to dispense with search warrants and allow the prosecutor the power to subpoena evidence, as the grand jury can, with no prior showing that it is connected to some criminal activity? Once we see clearly that we are giving the subpoena power to prosecutors, we may want to place limitations and conditions on it and, thus, prevent our accusatorial system from becoming an inquisitorial one.

Whence, however, have come the cautions against abolition, even by current critics of the grand jury? Those sensitive to the importance of the liberties enshrined in the Bill of Rights feel that the demand for greater control and conformity now cloaked in "law and order" signals is particularly intense at this time, and that any tinkering with the Bill of Rights might be met with a wholesale demand that we go further and alter many other guarantees of fundamental liberties, merely to gain "efficiency." They are, therefore, loath to begin "experimenting" and, thus, treating these constitutional provisions as if they had no more stature than legislation.

To the extent that this concern proceeds from a principled basis, a respect for the tradition embodied in the Constitution, and an appreciation of the wise perception of the founding fathers as to the arena of liberty individuals must have vis-à-vis the state, then their arguments must be given credence. To the extent, however, that these arguments are merely tactical, they have less weight if they suggest that we should tolerate a useless and destructive institution merely because others *might* use abolition of the grand jury as an opening for an attack against other protective and important constitutional provisions. Those who give this caution would hardly have been dissuaded from seeking a constitutional amendment if, for example, the Supreme Court had not eliminated capital punishment by declaring it unconstitutional. Capital punishment, a barbaric practice serving no social interests, should have been ended, even if by means of a constitutional amendment.

Therefore, the grand jury as an institution is supportable only if, independent of a "domino theory" about the dangers of trying to amend the Constitution, it has saving graces and can be made to serve the citizenry in the manner and for the purposes intended.

# XVI.

---

## Preserving the Grand Jury and Protecting Civil Liberties

The grand jury has some features with sufficient positive potential to warrant a serious effort at reforming the institution while concurrently placing controls on it so as to prevent abuses. Lay citizen involvement in government institutions is an important ingredient when it can prevent government agencies from hardening into bureaucracies that operate only on their own internal dynamic, ignoring that their only *raison d'être* is service to people. Criminal prosecution can have such devastating consequences for the convicted person that this may be a government function peculiarly in need of the tempering that ordinary citizens exercising common sense and skepticism bring to bear.

Petit trial juries have meted out this kind of humanizing community mitigation and, thus, have nullified prosecutions time after time against people whom the state sought to stamp as "dangerous" radicals. Defendants have been acquitted of the most serious charges against them in the Chicago conspiracy trial, the Bobby Seale trial in New Haven, the trial of the Black Panther 21 in New York, the Angela Davis trial, the trial of the Vietnam Veterans Against the War in Gainesville, Florida, and many others.

It is also good that grand jurors are taken out of their ordinary role at citizens and given an active piece of governmental responsibility. We are beginning to believe that government should not always be something that is done *to* or *for* citizens but should, where feasible, involve them in formulating and shaping policies that affect their lives.

It would be unwise, therefore, to move too quickly to excise citizen involvement in the criminal process at the very time when we are trying to realize the benefits from citizen intervention in so many other areas formerly given over totally to government officials. This is especially true since 1968 legislation promises to democratize the selection of people who sit on the grand jury.[1] The new law requires jurors to be chosen randomly from voter rolls, and outlaws the system in which panelists were chosen by ex-grand jurors, city officials, and law enforcement authorities. The old manner of selection resulted in grand juries composed of a narrow spectrum of middle-class, middle-aged white men.

Giving ordinary people policy-making roles has certainly been the trend in the experiments with community controlled school boards and new legal service programs. Crime control is governmental decision making that affects all citizens, and it behooves us to direct some of the public anxiety on this issue toward some constructive ends. The prime question, then, is, Can the grand jury be reformed to realize the benefits of citizen involvement and, most important, can we produce in the grand jurors an appropriate sense that they have a unique role, independent from that of the prosecutor? We shall return to the latter problem in a later chapter.

Reform should be tried at this time because, even if one were convinced that abolition of the grand jury was absolutely necessary, the process of constitutional amendment could take a substantial amount of time and would be resisted strenuously by those who still have faith in the institution. In the interim, we should make reforms that are more immediately realizable, and actively monitor the results of those reforms to make a more definitive judgment about the total worth of the institution.

The most immediate and important changes require placing controls on the grand jury to prevent the abuses of civil liberties that have recently characterized its operation. The first task is to stop the prosecutor from using the grand jury solely at his whim for harassment and disruption of political groups. The statement that the grand jury can begin its investigation solely on the basis of "tips [and] rumors"* is an absurdity and should be put to rest. If a prosecutor were ever mindless enough to state publicly that the expensive and time-consuming process of a grand jury investigation was begun solely on the basis of stray rumors or "hunches," he would probably be forced to resign by the resultant public protest. Since in fact this is a limited resource that should not be used haphazardly, it would be useful to formalize standards for instituting an investigation. Initially, the U.S. attorney could be required to show to a court, in order to subpoena witnesses, that there was reason to conduct the investigation. He should have to explain the kind of investigation intended, the kind of criminal activity prompting it, and the reasons for believing that the people and material he wishes to subpoena will aid that investigation. This would not require satisfying the standard of showing "probable cause" that a crime had been committed, which is required at the more formal prelimi-

---

*Costello v. United States*, 350 U.S. 359, 362 (1955).

nary hearing stage; he would simply have to convince the judge that the investigation was reasonable on the whole.

When the information supplied the court by the U.S. attorney indicated that the investigation would substantially intrude into First Amendment areas of political association and political beliefs, a higher standard would be required of the prosecution. It might then be necessary to have the prosecution show "probable cause" for believing that a crime had been committed in order to establish that there is a sufficiently important governmental interest justifying the intrusion on First Amendment rights.

Requiring the prosecution to limit and delineate before the court its arena for investigation would give a witness the option of having the court examine the questions potentially violating First Amendment rights and allow the witness not to answer questions irrelevant to the investigation as the U.S. attorney had outlined it.*

ABOLISH COMPULSORY PROCESS?

Requiring the prosecution to make some showing that the investigation is bona fide and based on evidence that a crime has occurred places no unreasonable burden on the prosecution. When there are no extraneous political motivations involved, most cases do have such evidence. Indeed, to the extent that the standards thus far suggested are hardly stringent, "bad faith" prosecutors could still use the grand jury to invade the privacy and political associations of witnesses. Political activity, especially that of a very intense and serious nature, usually raises borderline questions of legality. This is so because the law, to some extent,

---

*These suggestions are detailed in an excellent article by David J. Fine, "Federal Grand Jury Investigations of Political Dissidents," 7 Harv. Civil Rights, Civil Liberties L. Rev. 432, pp. 481-484 (1972).

generally requires conformity and uniformity, and those who administer the law seem to tolerate only the most circumspect and careful (read slow and ineffective) methods of changing the status quo. Activity for social change that entails making a new demand, or making an old demand with new methods and techniques, often gets an "illegal" label at first. Much protest activity over the past fifteen years has been so characterized—be it sit-ins to protest racial segregation in the South, student demonstrations at Kent State University, or Quakers taking medical supplies to North Vietnam during the war. When there appear to be no statutes appearing directly to make the activity criminal or unlawful, prosecutors with inventive minds merely patch together some charges and theories on which to base them. In the Pentagon Papers case, Solicitor General Erwin Griswold subsequently admitted that there was "no law" authorizing the government to stop *The New York Times* from publishing material, even when it was classified as secret. The government simply argued that the President, as Commander in Chief, had inherent power to do any thing necessary to protect "the public interest" against a grave danger. There was also strong argument that Daniel Ellsberg's transmittal of the papers to *The New York Times* was not specifically covered by any espionage legislation, but this did not deter the government from its strenuous prosecution.[2] The Supreme Court denied the government the right to stop publication of the Pentagon Papers on the basis of "no law," and the Ellsberg case never resolved the question of the legality of his prosecution because the government had engaged in its own illegal acts, which were *clearly* prohibited.

Given the minimal standards suggested, a prosecutor could still pry into much legitimate, and fundamentally legal, activity of a political nature. The courts have even recognized that the grand jury of necessity invades privacy, but that collateral consequence must be tolerated in order for it to perform its investigative function. One suggestion that would protect political activity more fully would simultaneously require us to reduce the coercive power of the grand jury and, consequently, to rely more on non-grand jury police investigations for crime control. The approach would be to leave the decision about testifying solely up to the witness, so that if he thought the prosecutor were simply trying to find out the structure, membership, and goals of a legitimate organization, unconnected to any bona fide criminal investigation, he could refuse to answer. Some recently proposed legislation goes partly in this direction by giving a witness the option to accept immunity from prosecution or to refuse to answer potentially incriminating questions. While such a proposal is respectful of the spirit of the Fifth Amendment privilege not to incriminate oneself, it leaves two substantial problems: First, it does not protect the witness who simply does not want to divulge information about his political alliances, even though divulging such information is not self-incriminating or even incriminating of others. Second, it creates the paradoxical situation of a witness' being unable to invoke the Fifth Amendment (when the questions are directed solely at the activity of others and would produce no incriminating evidence against him) while being subjected to jail for noncooperation in testifying about others. Such a witness, totally innocent of any criminal activity, might resist such questioning solely out of fear. Jail for an innocent but frightened person contrasts not so nicely with freedom for one who may in fact have committed an offense but could not be jailed for contempt because he is allowed to refuse to accept immunity. The only answer to all of these problems, and the one that promises the most effective protection of the rights to privacy and free association, would be to absolve *all* people from compulsory testimony, no matter what the subject of the inquiry. Indictments would then have to be based on evidence obtained through ordinary police investigations or through testimony secured voluntarily or by means of coercions other than the contempt sanction.

Initially, this proposal may seem foolhardy or too great a price to pay to free individuals and groups from governmental harassment, which some may say was an aberration tied to one administration. Prosecutors, for example, regularly claim that compulsory process is absolutely essential in criminal investigations. Its efficacy might be persuasive if, for example, it could be demonstrated that it was a key means of penetrating organized crime. The grand jury was around long before the development of well-organized criminal syndicates, but the President's Commission on Law Enforcement and Administration of Justice (hereafter Crime Commission) admitted in 1967 that "efforts to curb the growth of organized crime in America have not been successful."[3] The largest organized crime syndicate (the Mafia, or La Cosa Nostra) has an estimated membership of 3000–5000. Between 1960 and 1969, only 235 indictments were returned involving 328 alleged members of the organization, and this even after the Centralized Strike Force was established at the Justice Department to bear down on organized crime.[4] The reasons the Commission offered for this relative failure rate show why the grand jury is not, in this context, the "racket buster" of legend: The principals of the Mafia will not buckle under, even with a grant of immunity or jailings for contempt, to tell all about the internal workings of the organization. This is not surprising, for the Mafia credo of absolute obedience to its hierarchy and noncooperation with police authorities is extremely strong and maintained even during its own murderous internal warfare.

The most famous, massive, and ineffective use of the grand jury against La Cosa Nostra occurred around the

meeting of approximately 39 of the top leaders of the organization in Apalachin, New York, in 1957. Most of the people attending the meeting were called before grand juries on 27 occasions and were questioned by the FBI on 29 occasions, but gave no testimony that could be used directly to prove the criminal purpose of the meeting. Seven refused to talk even though they were granted immunity, and were held in jail for seven months for contempt. Despite the fact that the government had no direct evidence of any criminal purpose, it charged 20 of those attending with conspiracy to "defraud the United States" and to commit perjury. The convictions of all defendants were reversed on appeal. The court said that the jury could not be allowed to assume that the defendants were lying simply because they gave testimony that was not helpful in uncovering an illegal purpose* for the meeting and the government had no independent proof of such illegal purpose. The concurring judge outlined the total futility of the repeated grand jury inquiries and berated the prosecutor for even bringing the charges.

Mafia discipline is reinforced against outsiders, as with any highly organized crime ring, by the readiness to torture or assassinate possible informers. It is estimated that between 1961 and 1965, 25 informants against the Mafia were eliminated.[5] Such murders are facilitated by the fact that La Cosa Nostra is a national organization, thus allowing any local group under surveillance to import a "hit man" from a distant city to do the killing. Thus, the 18-month sentence for contempt before the grand jury is unlikely to make a potential witness testify who fears death at the hands of this gang.

Even victims in need of protection against extortionists are afraid to inform law enforcement authorities. More-

*United States v. Bufalino, 285 F. 408 (1960).

over, these victims and other potential witnesses have first-hand knowledge of the Crime Commission's conclusion that "organized crime flourishes where it has corrupted local officials."[6] Their fear of appearing before the grand jury is connected with the fear that someone in the prosecutor's office could be "reached" and report back to the organization. Even cooperative informers who do not fear furnishing intelligence to the law enforcement officials often condition it on their not being required to expose themselves at a public trial. Such informers obviously have limited usefulness if the prosecutor needs their testimony to secure a conviction.

The Crime Commission, while recognizing that the "wall of silence . . . often defeats the efforts of law enforcement to obtain live witnesses in organized crime cases,"[7] does argue that compulsory process is important in combatting organized crime. Its report recognizes, however, that the grand jury would have to be modified substantially if it were to be an effective ingredient of that attack.

The Commission proposed a number of changes in the grand jury that were subsequently adopted in the Organized Crime Control Act of 1970.[8] For example, a special grand jury must now be convened at least once every 18 months in heavily populated judicial districts to receive evidence of organized crime activity. The U.S. attorney conducting this proceeding is required to transmit to the grand jury any information a citizen wants it to receive on organized crime.* The grand jury can request an ex-

---

*There may be more of an appearance of grand jury independence here than will obtain in practice. First, because of the secrecy of the grand jury, a citizen who transmits information to a corrupt local prosecutor will never know whether it in fact reached the grand jury. Second, the prosecutor can make recommendations to the grand jurors as to whether the information so transmitted is worth considering. The grand jury may generally accept the prosecutor's evaluation.

tension of its time of services for a maximum of 36 months
if its investigation is incomplete; if the local district court
judge attempts to terminate the investigation before its
completion, the grand jurors can secure authorization from
the chief judge of the circuit to stay in session. Obviously,
these changes are designed to prevent any corrupt U.S.
attorney or local judge from blocking or suppressing an
investigation.

Perjury convictions can be secured more easily under
the new legislation, and a special grand jury may issue a
report criticizing any public official for laxity or malfeasance, short of criminal conduct, in the pursuit of organized
crime. Such a public official has an opportunity to rebut
such charges before the report is made public. The grand
jury may also report on general conditions in its area with
respect to organized crime, but without identifying any
private citizen.

These legislative changes are the product of some well-
considered reports on organized crime, and certainly the
impact deserves close study. Most of the reforms go toward
neutralizing corrupt officials; few are responsive to the most
pressing problem—the intense fear of potential witnesses.*
Electronic surveillance and tax evasion charges, which may
be proved through documentary evidence, are claimed to be
significant prosecutorial tools against organized crime, but
most people writing on organized crime say that live wit-

*Some have claimed that the changes will have little impact on
*federal* prosecutions because most corruption by organized crime
has been traced primarily to state and municipal officials. The
centralization of the organized crime strike forces is said to have
further diminished the potential for corruption, at least of the
federal prosecutor. However, data show that organized crime
figures have escaped conviction at a much higher rate than other
defendants. While this acquittal rate may be a reflection of
other factors (e.g., good defense lawyers), it does argue for adopting all lawful measures possible to deter influence purchasing.

nesses are absolutely essential for any major assault. The only part of the new legislation that directly addresses the problem of protecting witnesses is that which authorizes the attorney general to offer residence in a federally guarded facility to any witness and his family.

Close examination of the 1970 Act leads to the speculation that it will have an impact only in very specialized circumstances, and that in almost *no* case will the specific sanctions attached to the compulsory process of the grand jury overcome the strong and realistic fears of witnesses.

The range and spectrum of potential witnesses, and their specific circumstances, reveal why compulsory process may be ineffective. First, the person willing to testify against an organized ring rarely does so on the basis of being public spirited; the norm, even when the crimes are not so serious and the threat of retaliation is less overt, is that citizens avoid getting "involved." But some strong motivation (e.g., a mob murder of a relative, or wanting to stop his own extortion) might make a witness willing to testify, and the protection of the federal facility may be the additional assurance needed. Such a person testifies primarily for personal and independent reasons, *not* because he could be compelled to appear before the grand jury. Even with such compulsory process, what does it mean for the particular witness? He and his family, if he has one, must be moved not only into the federal facility pending the completion of the trial but also permanently out of the community in which they formerly lived. When Robert Kennedy was attorney general, he promised witnesses just such protected relocation, but still relatively few indictments of organized crime members resulted during that period.

As for the ordinary law-abiding citizen, the grand jury and other coercive measures available to law officials seem irrelevant or ineffective in securing his cooperation. First, such a person is not likely to possess any crucial information

about an operation that is well structured, clandestine, and highly resistant even to the planting of informers. Second, if by some fortuitous circumstance such a person has become privy to information against an organized ring, is he likely to run the risk of public testimony and accept, as a matter of public duty, the necessity of totally changing life patterns and relocating to another community? Upon any refusal to give information and the prosecutor's being convinced that the witness has not personally been involved in criminal activities but is genuinely fearful, would he seek to jail him for contempt? If the witness testifies, and suddenly has "amnesia" for the events or misrepresents the facts, again, will the prosecutor feel sanguine about pressing for a perjury conviction with its concomitant five years of imprisonment?

Let us assume that the prosecutor has lined up another potential witness because of proof, independent of his testimony, that the witness *has* been involved in criminal activities. The "use" immunity statute was designed specifically with this kind of witness in mind. The prosecutor could force testimony from the witness while still holding out the possibility of conviction if the witness were not sufficiently cooperative and truthful. However, such a witness, because of his acquaintance with the underworld, is likely to be even more aware than the average citizen of the ruthlessness of those he may testify against and, thus, may decide that even imprisonment on a serious offense is better than running the risk of being murdered. The 18-month sentence for civil contempt, the maximum for refusing to testify before a special grand jury, is unlikely to change that assessment. Further, the witness may even decide to lie to avoid informing on mob members in the hope that the perjury will not be discovered and in the knowledge that even if it is, the 5-year sentence for perjury is still the safer option. *If* such a witness does testify, it will more likely be in order to avoid

conviction on his own, independent criminal offenses if
they carry very stiff sentences. In any event, compulsory
process of the grand jury is largely irrelevant with respect to
this witness, also.

Did we need the grand jury's compulsory process to
nail the public officials involved in Watergate? Did not
some of them subsequently plead guilty to perjury before
the grand jury, and how could this have happened unless
they were required to testify? This admittedly poses a hard
question, especially for the "Watergates" of the future,
since the public trust is, apparently, easily abused by people
in high governmental positions. However, the track record
of Watergate shows that none of the officials involved
absconded and none demanded immunity *in the grand jury*
as the *quid pro quo* for testifying. All participated voluntarily,* even though some lied. Giving up compulsion to
appear and testify, however, does not mean you must dis-
card the perjury offense—those who do testify must do so
truthfully or face the consequences. But how do we know
that these officials would have participated were there no
option to compel them to? Frankly, we do not know, but
perhaps public officials are too visible and vulnerable to
public opinion to risk refusing to appear. At the outset, these
public officials probably tried to deflect any suspicion from

---

*Nixon said he would not appear before a grand jury while he
occupied the Presidency, but there is a good argument that he
could not have been required to, even if a subpoena had been
served on him. Likewise, even though the court ruled that
Nixon had to acquiesce in a subpoena for his tapes, it is ques-
tionable as to how the order could have been enforced if Nixon
had ignored it. Ultimately, the impeachment process may be the
only way to deal with derelictions by a President. The topic,
however, is beyond the scope of this book, and suggestions are
being made here that at least appointed public officials can be
dealt with differently.

themselves and, thus, appeared and testified and did not demand immunity. To do otherwise would probably have brought the wrath of the public on them and pressure on the elected officials who had appointed them to dismiss them.

Indeed, since the primary public interest in such a matter *is* removal from office, it is possible that we could treat the public official differently from ordinary citizens. He has taken on a position of public trust, and therefore, special responsibility can be attached to it. We could still preserve for him the option that any other citizen would have of not being compelled to testify, but we could require the dismissal of a public official if he were uncooperative. This would not violate his constitutional right not to incriminate himself if we preserved the grant of immunity for any interrogation that implicated him personally. The suggestion is in keeping with other special demands for information that we place on public officials—such as the Freedom of Information Act, for which there is no equivalent in the private sector. We could leave elected officials to the judgment of the electorate in future elections.

This suggestion, obviously, does not deal with Watergate conspirators who were not public officials, but it is not asserted that there would be no costs to criminal investigations. All that is asserted is that we should now assess whether the compulsory subpoena has created other and more substantial costs that we should refuse to continue paying.

All of this analysis may be a bit too "rational" and speculative, since prosecutors invariably affirm the need for compelling testimony to combat organized crime, and it may not be accurate for *every* witness in the categories described. Yet all too often commentators simply assert that the compulsory process is effective against organized rings, but do not back up this claim with any specific studies that prove the proposition.* The preceding exploration concerning the disutility of compulsory process in the context of organized crime may also prove, conversely, that it *can* be effective against nonorganized garden variety crime, in which the same threats to witnesses are not so palpable. It can be argued that it is especially needed in an urbanized, rural and town-dominated Americans, do not develop personal relationships that make them feel responsible for one another. In any urban area in any given year, we are visited with the spectacle of some citizens ignoring the cries of a fellow citizen for help when he is the butt of some kind of criminal attack. The grand jury subpoena may be a device for cutting down that kind of indifference and, indeed, compelling cooperation in sorting out information about the typical urban street offense.

In any event, the National Commission on Individual

*A classic example is Robert Blakey's report, "Aspects of the Evidence Gathering Process in Organized Crime Cases: A Preliminary Analysis," made for the Task Force on Organized Crime of the Crime Commission. After noting that witnesses are generally reluctant in organized crime investigations, he quotes Attorney General Nicholas de B. Katzenbach as saying that it had been necessary to forgo prosecution "hundreds of . . . . [times] because key witnesses would not testify for fear of [being murdered]." Blakey's next sentence is that "compulsory process is necessary" (at page 83), as if compulsory process could overcome the threat about which Katzenbach testified. Blakey later quotes from another article to the effect that "as an instrument of discovery against organized crime, the grand jury has no counterpart," citing Younger, "The Grand Jury Under Attack," 46 J. Crim. L.C. and P.S. 214, 224 (1955). A reading of Younger's article shows that it is merely an assertion with no reference to any data. Cases do the same thing—see *Levinson v. Attorney General* 321 F. Supp. 984 (1970), which cites another case for the proposition (*In re Grand Jury* 4 F. Supp. 283 (1933) —but a check of that case shows that this conclusion, too, is merely asserted, not documented.

Rights, set up by the Organized Crime Control Act, may answer some of these questions, because it is authorized to study the effectiveness of the special grand jury. Primarily a watchdog on potential civil liberty abuses, it has not yet issued a report, but it is hoped that it will also evaluate the utility of the changes made in the grand jury as an evidence gatherer against organized crime. Until such data are available, the proposal for a total ban on compulsory process is likely to be viewed with great skepticism. However, this is one of the key conflicts that runs throughout our look at the grand jury: How much are we willing to let an institution operate so as to intrude upon some of our most fundamental freedoms of privacy and political association because that institution can possibly be turned around and used against some antisocial elements in our society?

One can decide, on a value basis, to dispense with the immediate prosecutorial advantages, even if they are real, on the ground that there are some principles that transcend the increment of increased efficiency. This is especially true if one makes the judgment that the ultimate eradication of organized crime can never be achieved by slightly more efficient means of prosecution but, rather, only through major structural reforms in the society at large. The energy for, and conception of, such reforms may emerge from the very radical groups that the government may try to suppress, using the grand jury as one of its weapons. It behooves the public at large and those in positions of responsibility to that public to consider seriously diminishing the coercive uses of tools that have been subverted in the name of "crime control."

SECRECY AND THE GRAND JURY

Even were one not to accept a rule entirely barring compulsory testimony, we could modify grand jury procedure slightly so as to diminish the divisive impact on the new stripe of political activist of being called before a grand jury. Grand jury secrecy is premised primarily on the problems presented in an investigation into organized crime or political corruption. None of the interests normally protected by secrecy would in fact be protected in the typical investigation of political dissidents. First, an attempt to prevent an about-to-be indicted suspect from fleeing will not work because witnesses are usually his political allies and will alert him that the investigation is focusing on him, especially since they can discuss what went on in the sessions they have attended without violating any grand jury rule. Thus, the prosecution will have to use some other means of controlling the accused while the investigation is under way (e.g., surveillance or arrest).

Second, the notion that unindicted and innocent people will be spared adverse publicity is also belied by the fact that a witness can go straight to the newspapers and talk about the investigation. The McCarthy Committee hearings into "subversive activity" were objectionable because they were designed to expose an unpopular minority to a public that was ready to penalize them; however, new-style activists would welcome a public platform (*à la* Chicago conspiracy trial) from which to expose government methods as "oppressive." They have learned to make publicity work for and not against them. Third, a witness who testifies about his political associates is not usually concerned about reprisals but is more concerned that they do not distrust him because he has talked to the authorities in private.

One need not, however, demand that all grand jury proceedings be conducted in public—we can simply give the witness a full transcript of his testimony, which he could then share with others. As stated earlier, one court has held that a witness can resist testifying if the government refuses to make a transcript available; however, this was based on a strained reading of the publication rules that control grand jury proceedings, and new legislation would, thus, be more appropriate. This would, naturally, require all grand jury proceedings to be regularly transcribed—something that is already done in many jurisdictions.

## REPORTS FROM THE JUSTICE DEPARTMENT

A consequence of grand jury secrecy is that neither the courts nor Congress, nor, especially, the public, can gauge how the institution is being used. It was only through the efforts of groups like the Coalition Against Grand Jury Abuse that some public attention was focused on activation of the grand jury against political activists during the Nixon years. The activity of this group has provoked a number of legislative proposals to reform the grand jury; those submitted by Congressmen John Conyers and Charles Rangel would require the attorney general to report annually, describing the number and nature of all grand jury investigations and all proceedings collateral thereto, such as contempt, grants of immunity, and dismissals of prosecution. A most important requirement is disclosure of whether information received from the grand jury is being fed into data banks.* This, coupled with the requirement about reporting the outcome of investigations, might indicate whether the grand jury was being used for indictments or primarily for surveillance and compiling dossiers. The provisions are salutary in that they preserve anonymity for all defendants while exposing the priorities that the Justice Department is establishing in the use of the institution.

*The National Commission on Individual Rights has authority under the Organized Crime Control Act (1970) to gather such information.

INFORMING THE WITNESS OF CONSTITUTIONAL RIGHTS

Other legislation would reduce the vulnerability of witnesses before the grand jury. Congressman Eilberg proposed that a witness be given adequate and reasonable notice of his right against self-incrimination, the nature of the grand jury investigation, whether he is a potential defendant, and most important, that he has a right to counsel. The Conyers bill specifically allows the witness' attorney to be present in the grand jury room. This should be interpreted as limiting counsel to advising the witness with respect to questions put to him, but barring any further participation so that critics of this reform cannot claim that the grand jury would be unable to function swiftly because it was being turned into a minitrial. Indeed, the proposal, so limited, could be more efficient than the practice that now prevails in which the witness has to ask to leave the room to consult with counsel. Some have said that the witness may lose a benefit of the present practice—he at least can talk confidentially with his attorney outside the grand jury room. This can be resolved, however, by defense counsel's asking to be excused on the few occasions when further private consultation is needed. In general, it will be better for the witness' counsel to be present to counteract the dominance that the prosecutor now exercises over the proceedings.

One hallmark of the government's use of the grand jury as a "fishing expedition" is the failure to return an indictment. To deter this, the government should be required to pay attorney's fees to witnesses who have retained counsel (or the organizations that have supplied counsel gratis) when no prosecution results. This can prevent the government from using the grand jury to deplete the resources of a group it is trying to harass.

If we grant a witness a right to counsel, it is integral to that right that he have time to consult with him. The practice of serving a subpoena at 7 A.M. on a witness to report before the grand jury at 10 A.M. the same day, as was done with Daniel Ellsberg's 15-year-old son, should be prohibited. In the absence of an emergency, such tactics are designed solely to panic the witness and prevent a considered evaluation of his rights. Grand jury investigations are planned and arranged by the prosecutor, so adequate advance notice to the witness of 7 to 10 days should be possible in most cases. The prosecutor should be required to show that there is an emergency if he wants someone on less notice.

# XVII.

_____

## Grand Jury Reform: Newsmen, Scholars, and Government Officials' Privilege

The Bay of Pigs fiasco, the Vietnam War, and Watergate, involving three successive Presidents and both political parties, should be occasions enough to convince us of the danger of government functionaries' abusing the public trust by covertly adopting policies that do not serve the interest of the average citizen. A watchdog press and skeptical public officials may be our only vanguard for penetrating the self-justifying falsifications that are integral to government attempts to negate or suppress public debate. As Justice Douglas so eloquently put it,

> The story of the Pentagon Papers is a chronicle of suppression of vital decisions to protect the reputations and political hides of men who worked an amazingly successful scheme of deception on the American people. They were successful not because they were astute but because

the press had become a frightened, regimented, submissive instrument, fattening on favors from those in power and forgetting the great tradition of reporting. To allow the press further to be cowed by grand jury inquiries and prosecution is to carry the concept of "abridging" the press to frightening proportions.*

The enormity of government malfeasance alone might justify protecting outside critics from counterattack by way of subpoena, for the errors of negligence or, more likely, the "hidden agendas" have cost thousands of lives and billions of dollars. In that event, however, it might be only appropriate to fit the remedy to the evil—namely, to immunize newsmen, scholars and antiadministration officials only when they are reporting on government operations. However, non-governmentally sponsored crime is a serious problem, in part because so much fear has been generated in the public because of it. We may never be able to utilize the most efficient unit for living—the urban center—unless we find ways to cope with crime, either in fact or in perception.

But people must be alert to what is going on with respect to ordinary criminal activity before we can begin to think through the measures necessary to suppress or deter it in the future.** Newsmen and scholars should not be

*Gravel v. United States,* 408 U.S. 606, at pp. 648-649.

**Congress has recognized this fact as regards the drug problem. Researchers in this field can be required to disclose the identity of their subjects only upon a showing of good cause to a court— Drug Abuse Office and Treatment Act of 1972 (Pub. L. No. 92-255, 86 Stat. 66—codified in scattered sections of 5, 21, 42, U.S.C.). A previous, unrepealed statute made the privilege absolute— Comprehensive Drug Abuse Prevention and Control Act of 1970 (Pub. L. No. 91-513, 84 Stat. 1236—codified in sections of 18, 21, 26, 31, 40, 42. 46, 49, U.S.C.), and one case applied it despite the more recent enactment *People v. Newman,* 32 N.Y. 2d. 379 (1973).

turned into de facto undercover policemen if this seriously diminishes the knowledge people must have to jog their democratic institutions into a response. Admittedly, this presents society with a very difficult value choice—information versus apprehension. The choice need not be all or none. We can compromise by, for example, permitting subpoenas when the prosecution can assert that the information is needed to prevent a threat to human life, or espionage and foreign aggression.*

The privilege of the newsman or government official not to be subpoenaed to the grand jury should be tied to the goal of informing the public under legitimate and appropriate circumstances. It should not extend to the source of any information concerning the details of any grand jury proceeding that was required to be secret. As stated previously, such disclosures could substantially prejudice the right of a person subsequently indicted to a fair and unbiased trial, and the question for the news media is only *when* the public will be informed, not *whether* it will be informed.

An exception to the newsman's privilege not to produce material should be made for any that has already been made public. The informing function has been discharged, and the only question remaining is whether the prosecution is to have evidence in its most reliable form. Such information could be captured by the law enforcement officials at the time it was made public, if they were alerted, and thus, it seems hard to suggest that because they were not so alerted they cannot have the material. There is no problem

*This is not a major concession, for even without a statute granting a privilege, such crimes are unlikely to be the direct focus of empirical research. Newsmen in the Blasi study generally said that they felt they would not promise anyone anonymity in such emergency circumstances. An elected official would court certain defeat if he withheld evidence in such cases.

here concerning newspapers, books, and magazines, which can be secured without using the publisher, but it has come up in connection with televised programs and radio broadcasts based on tapes. Even in that instance, there would seem to be no difficulty when the newsman procures the information without having a confidential relationship with the person filmed or recorded. Newsmen, for example, have filmed brutality by policemen engaging in arrests in the Watts riots and guards securing a house of detention in New York City after a prisoner riot.

The tougher question is illustrated by the battle between Station WBAI in New York City and law enforcement officials. The station made recordings of prisoners after they had seized guards as hostages in the Tombs Prison and subsequently broadcast these statements. Turning the tapes over to law enforcement officials would have undercut the promises of confidentiality that were made because voice prints could be used in a prosecution for identification purposes.\* The radio station probably sought to achieve a greater quality of authenticity by letting the public hear

---

\*The case might come under the exception to the newsman's privilege when there is a serious threat to human life, even after the hostages had been released, if we do not require the threat to be "immediate." A claim can be made that prison guards are in jeopardy in the future as long as the inmates who led the riot are not put in maximum security facilities or under special surveillance. For example, George Jackson, author of the famed "Soledad Brother," is supposed to have given a tape to his editor admitting that he had murdered a prison guard. Jackson subsequently attempted a jail break in which he was killed—*Village Voice*, May 16, 1974, p. 1, col. 1. One could argue against forcing the newsman to turn over his tapes because there is the alternative of the released guards' identifying their captors. However, the fact that particular prisoners could be identified as the active ones on the tape, would provide an incentive to release the guards unharmed.

the prisoners' actual statements rather than summaries. However, this should be resolved by the reporter's explaining to his sources the risk they run if they authorize him to broadcast the material as recorded. If they wish to reach the public, but do not wish simultaneously to ensure their own conviction, the station should give only a summarized, anonymous version, and the recorded statements (taken to ensure an accurate summary) should not be subject to subpoena.

Aside from these qualifications, newsmen and congressmen ought to have an absolute privilege not to disclose any information that they have received confidentially, in their professional capacity, and not made public. Nor should they be required to disclose an unidentified *source* of any information, whether published or not. Since such legislation would give the reporter the *privilege* not to testify, presumably he could choose to do so voluntarily. This introduces a measure of uncertainty for the source of the information, for he then is totally reliant on the newsman to keep his word. If we truly want people to feel absolutely free to communicate with the public through news media or their congressmen, we should require a newsman or congressman to swear that the *source* has authorized a disclosure of his name. The privilege then would belong, not to an "elite" corps of journalists, but to average people who have newsworthy information they want to get to the public, but who need the assurance of anonymity to do so.* Although there may be constitutional problems because of our separate federal and state systems,[1] it is suggested here that federal legislation cover both federal and state grand juries because the increased resort to newsmen has occurred in both bodies. Federal and state criminal laws often over-

*The State of Alaska has a statute adopting this approach. Alaska Stat. sec. 09.25 150-.220

lap; thus, while a newsman might be immune from sub-poena before a federal grand jury, if his stories also touch on state offenses, any local state prosecutor could subpoena him where there is no state shield law. This could leave the news media as inhibited as if there were no federal legisla-tion, because news gathering and dissemination often has an interstate character.

# XVIII.

---

# Reform of
the Grand Jury:
The Average
Witness
or Defendant

The foregoing chapters are aimed at harmonizing and integrating the grand jury with other provisions of the Bill of Rights. If adopted, fundamental freedoms to political beliefs, association, and right to privacy could be protected to a greater extent, and political activity, that constant goad to change that is so necessary in a healthy democracy, would be buffered against governmental suppression.

Reforms for the grand jury—undefined and unrestrained as it has been—could protect the average citizen finding himself a witness or a target of its criminal investigation. Such reforms can have the indirect effect of protecting free speech and free association, for the clarification of uncharted areas of discretion by explicit standards makes it easier for potential victims to resort to the courts for relief.

For example, poor people usually do not have a right

to appointment of counsel at the expense of the state until they have been arrested or formally indicted. The result is that, at present, only people with sufficient financial resources or with none, the latter assisted by an organization like the National Lawyers Guild or the American Civil Liberties Union, have had lawyers at grand jury proceedings. Counsel should be made available to all indigents called to the grand jury, even when they are only witnesses and not suspects, for the proceedings can be fraught with serious legal questions and consequences. This availability need not be financially burdensome for the government, because witnesses with no reluctance to testify and no fear of incriminating themselves will, in most instances, not ask for continuous legal representation. However, the government should provide a defense lawyer to advise *every* witness not represented by counsel as to whether a lawyer could assist him, given his particular circumstances.

A conviction can occur only after a trial based on competent and admissible evidence. Therefore, the present grand jury practice of introducing hearsay, material seized in violation of the Fourth Amendment, and other incompetent evidence not admissible at trial should be prohibited. We are now on a patchwork path: barring illegally seized wiretaps from being used in the grand jury, while allowing all other illegally seized evidence to be used; allowing a defendant to invoke his Fifth Amendment right not to give verbal evidence in support of conviction, but not his Fourth Amendment right to withhold tangible evidence unless some foundation can be laid linking it to a crime. The suggestion for reform made here would correct such anomalies and enhance the primary function of the grand jury—preventing trial of people against whom the prosecution lacks competent proof of guilt.

Tightening the evidentiary standards of the grand jury further is possible only if the defendant has a right to a transcript of the entire grand jury proceedings, since only he will have a stake in enforcing the rules barring improper evidence. At present, a defendant may get a transcript of his own testimony before the grand jury,[1] and of that of other witnesses upon a showing of "particularized need" after they testify at trial.[2] If he wishes the entire transcript prior to trial, he must show that grounds exist for dismissing the indictment. An exception to the requirement of disclosure to the defendant could be made for evidence that would endanger the national security or expose informers whose identities the government wishes to keep secret. The grand jury is now a unilateral means for the prosecutor to secure evidence. Given the much greater investigative resources the prosecutor already has (police, FBI, etc.) in contrast to the defense, access to the total transcript of the grand jury proceedings merely gives the defendant a fairer, more efficient, and timely opportunity to refute the charges against him.* Withholding disclosure of a witness' grand jury testimony until he has testified at trial gives the defendant no time to conduct an investigation for adequate cross-examination.

The traditional reasons for keeping the proceedings secret have little substance once the defendant is indicted. For example, if there is fear that the defendant may attempt to escape after assessing the strength of the prosecutor's case by reading the transcript before trial, bail could be raised in order to discourage flight.** The concern about the disclosure of information harmful to reputations of unindicted innocent people obviously has no relevance to a defendant who is being publicly charged. If there is transcript material

---

*The suggestion has been made in a report of the A.B.A. Special Committee on Federal Rules of Procedure, 38 F.R.D. 94, 106 (1965).

***United States v. Melville.*

irrelevant to the defendant's defense, but possibly embarrassing to innocent people if publicized, it should be deleted. Or, when relevant, the defendant and his lawyer could be put under penalty of contempt if they disclose such material beyond that necessary to prepare a defense. There should be no fear about bribery or harassing of witnesses to lie, because they have testified under oath and run the risk of a perjury charge if they change their testimony at trial. But if perjury charges seem an insufficient deterrent against a possible change in testimony, because the defendant or his confederates might attempt to intimidate the witness before the trial, protective custody could be provided. Likewise, there need be no fear that the grand jurors' deliberations will be disclosed, for the defendant would be entitled to only the testimony of witnesses. Consistent with other provisions for indigent parties, the government should supply the transcript at no cost.

## LEGISLATING AN ANTI-"DOUBLE JEOPARDY"
## PROVISION FOR THE GRAND JURY

Even if the letter of the Constitution bars conviction of a person twice for the same offense only when a conviction for contempt is criminal and not "civil," we should enact legislation that adopts the spirit of the double jeopardy provisions. If a witness is jailed for refusal to testify about a particular transaction, it should be unlawful to jail him a second time for refusal to give information on the same subject matter, especially since civil and criminal contempt overlap and can, in some instances, be applied to the same conduct. Repeated confinements for the same "civil" contempt may be barred by the constitutional provisions against "cruel and unusual punishments." The cases to date, however, have prohibited only very extreme types of punishment, like extended solitary confinement or the death penalty, so this constitutional limitation may not be an effective control on repeated incarceration.*

If we are not troubled by the doubtful constitutional validity of repeated jailings for refusal to answer the same questions, it may seem an attractive technique for use against the members of organized crime. Since it is extremely difficult to catch them at their primary criminal activity, why not put them in jail for contempt for not divulging that activity? We may have to tolerate repeated contempt sentences occasionally being used against other people, but perhaps it is worth that price if we can strike successfully at the dangerous leaders of organized crime.

That tack was tried in Chicago in 1965. U.S. Attorneys Sam Betar and David Schippers got Salvatore Giancanna, reputedly a leading crime figure, sent to jail for one year for refusing to answer questions. They were on their way toward a second jailing on the basis of the same questions when then Attorney General Ramsey Clark ordered a halt. The primary problem with the approach Betar and Schippers were pursuing is precisely its claimed merit: It amounts to jailing someone for offenses they are believed to have committed, *because* proof that they committed them is not available.

This is all the more true if a witness, like the typical high-level member of organized crime, has had much experience—from many arrests—at resisting interrogation. Such a candidate will rarely be coerced by short jail terms and, therefore, will not be a source of evidence. (Giancanna, given full transactional immunity, still refused to talk.) The Chicago case did not test out the proposition that this tactic may be unlawful; there are cases which say that if

*Furman v. Georgia* 408 U.S. 238 (1972) (Capital punishment) *Trop v. Dulles* 356 U.S. 86 (1957) (Loss of citizenship for wartime desertion); *Sostre v. McGinnis* 442 F. 2d 178 (2nd Cir. 1971) (Solitary confinement).

the court finds that the jailing is merely "punitive" and not
designed to get evidence, the contemnor can be freed.[3]

## POWER TO CHOOSE THE SITUS

Throughout the history of the grand jury, including recent
months, the unfettered discretion of the prosecutor to
choose the situs of the grand jury investigation has been
manipulated to enhance the possibilities of indictment.
Speculation was rife, for example, that Harrisburg, Pennsylvania, was chosen to investigate Daniel and Philip Berrigan and their associates on the Catholic Left because Harrisburg has a large, conservative, Catholic population that
would be hostile to the goals of such a group. Since there
are no controls on the situs of the grand jury, witnesses
have been required to travel thousands of miles from their
home base, away from family and friends, despite the fact
that most of what they are queried about usually occurred
in other parts of the country. Some of the ex-officials of the
Nixon administration made a similar claim of potential
prejudice of jurors when their trials were to be conducted
in Washington, D.C., with a predominantly Democratic
and black population that had voted against Nixon at an
85 per cent level. However, the situations are not compa-
rable because the trial, as opposed to the grand jury investigation, is not totally within the control of the prosecutor,
for it must be held where the offense was alleged to have
been committed. This still leaves some latitude for manipulation by the prosecutor, especially in conspiracy charges,
in which the offense may have occurred over a wide geo-
graphical area. However, a defendant has a formal and
recognized way of objecting to being tried in a prejudiced
atmosphere or community, and if the trial judge fails to
accede to an appropriate claim the conviction can be reversed on appeal. No such mechanism is available to people
called before the grand jury.

New and effective legislation should permit a witness to object, in a court located in the district of his residence, to being required to travel a long distance to another district if this would impose unnecessary hardship on him or his family. Derivatively, the court would have the power to order a transfer of the grand jury proceedings to the district best suited for investigation, depending on where most of the criminal activity is alleged to have occurred and on the residence of most of the parties to be called before the grand jury. If necessary, the court would also have the power to require the witness to give his testimony before a grand jury in the district of residence, with a transcript being submitted to the grand jury where most of the testimony will be taken. (This recommendation, however, has the disadvantage of the grand jurors in the main proceedings not being able to evaluate the demeanor of the witness; but if such observation appears to be a crucial factor from the viewpoint of the prosecution, perhaps that might be an occasion for requiring the witness to travel and make a personal appearance.)

# XIX.

---

# Building
# an Independent
# Grand Jury

Much of the complaint that the grand jury has become useless is based on its dominance by the prosecutor and the consequent passivity of the jurors. Citizen involvement can be meaningful only if it is active over and beyond voting solely on whether to indict.

The issuance of subpoenas, the request that a witness be granted immunity or held in contempt could all be voted upon by some portion of the grand jury.* The court, not the prosecutor, could at the outset of each grand jury proceeding be required to inform the grand jurors of such powers, along with its additional right to interrogate wit-

*The Conyers bill suggests a vote of 12 of the 23 grand jurors. Giving the grand jury these powers assumes that there has been no legislation that abolishes compulsory process, as suggested in Chapter XVI.

nesses.* The court should also take the opportunity to explain to the group its historic role as grand jury, especially its shielding protection for innocent people, including those against whom the government may have some special animus. If the judge has failed to give these instructions, a witness who refuses to testify should be free of contempt charges, and the indictment should be subject to dismissal. The obvious objective of these modifications is to invest in grand jurors a sense of their responsibility for, and control over, the process. Grand jurors would make many of the decisions now made by the prosecutor alone.

If grand jurors are to take more seriously their screening and protective function, the indicting and investigatory functions should be separated. We could grant the federal prosecutor power to subpoena witnesses outside the presence of the grand jury, so that he alone would conduct the initial exploratory investigations to see if there was a case. Only when he had developed sufficient information to warrant indictment would he bring the matter before the grand jury for consideration. This suggestion would absolve the grand jurors of the difficult task of being investigators and then having to shift to evaluating the evidence. Having the sole function of screening might also encourage

*If the grand jury could receive only evidence admissible at trial, it would be wise to have the grand jurors submit their questions to the prosecutor in advance, when possible, so that he could advise them about their proper form and permissibility. The prosecutor's role here, however, should be advisory. If the grand juror still wishes to ask the question, it should be submitted to the court when there is time for its ruling. If the grand jurors wish to interrogate witnesses without the prior opportunity to submit their questions to the prosecutor and he thinks that some improper questions were asked during the session, he could ask for a ruling from the court, and have the court instruct the grand jurors not to consider evidence based on such improper questioning. The prosecutor's incentive to do this would be the protection of the indictment against possible dismissal.

grand jurors to perceive their role as independent from the prosecutor's. Much grand juror time would be saved, for they would not have to sit passively while the prosecutor scans testimony to see if it is worthwhile to go further and seek more evidence.

Such changes would require no constitutional amendment, only congressional legislation.* The single potential problem is the *Miranda* case, which permits a suspect being held under legal compulsion to remain mute. This suggests that if the federal prosecutor is to have investigative subpoena power outside of the grand jury context, he should be required to inform a person whom he intends to charge of his right not to respond at all. However, *Miranda* probably is not applicable to the kind of prosecutor interrogation here envisioned, and the suspect could be required to answer all non-self-incriminating questions. *Miranda* was directed primarily at reducing for a recently arrested suspect, the inherently coercive atmosphere of incommunicado interrogation in a police station, since that had often been the situs of physical or mental coercion aimed at forcing confessions. Thus, the right to absolute silence would not apply, especially if the reforms suggested earlier were adopted (party informed of right to counsel, adequate time for consultation, right not to incriminate himself, etc.), because the court could find that interrogation in a controlled, transcribed proceeding had none of the coercive features that *Miranda* sought to neutralize. Further, the court in *Miranda* did not freeze interrogation into a fixed mold; rather, it explicitly invited Congress to legislate alternatives, as long as they provided the same basic protections that the court's formula sought to establish.

The heavy involvement of grand juries in the Water-

*A strong argument can be made that the framers of the Constitution never intended an active investigatory role for the grand jury. See David Fine, 7 Harv. Civil Rights, Civil Liberties L. Rev. 432, p. 443.

gate matter may leave an unwarranted impression that, in its present form, it is an effective instrument against government corruption. Watergate, however, teaches just the opposite: that a government prosecutor dominating the grand jury may not be aggressive or effective in pursuing the malfeasance of his superiors, or if he is independent enough to train his investigation on them, he may find himself abruptly retired from the position, as was Special Prosecutor Archibald Cox. The most explosive Watergate information did not come when regular prosecutors were conducting the grand jury investigations in the fall of 1972. It was only after Judge John Sirica, correctly assuming that the grand jury had not developed the full story, threatened the defendants discovered in the break-in at Democratic National Headquarters with stiff penalties. One of their number, James McCord, broke, and then the full story began to unravel. Indeed, two senators called for an inquiry into whether there had been a dereliction of duty on the part of Earl J. Silbert, who was in charge of the Watergate grand jury,[1] and it has been reported that an assistant attorney general (Henry Petersen) was transmitting information on occurrences in the grand jury to the White House under the claim that as head of the executive branch the President had a right of access to the testimony.[2] It may be all too easy to second-guess the decisions of these regular prosecutors, given subsequent disclosures, but much of their handling of the grand jury investigation raises serious doubts about their purposes. It has been claimed that the three-month delay between the arrest of the Watergate burglars and their indictment for a crime at which they were caught red-handed (June 17, 1972, to September 15, 1972) was inordinately long—precluding the embarrassment of a trial before the November 1972 elections. John W. Dean 3d was not called before the grand jury to testify, although the prosecutors were informed that he was supposed to have conducted a special investigation of the burglary for the White House. Despite the fact that some of the men arrested were employees of the Committee to Re-Elect the President, Maurice Stans, a major functionary of the Committee, was allowed to file a sworn, written statement in lieu of appearing before the grand jury and being cross-examined. The prosecutors did not try the case on the theory that the break-in was designed to surreptitiously secure information that could be used to enhance Nixon's chances for reelection, but on the notion that Gordon Liddy was the top organizer and that he was seeking to profit financially by using private conversations to blackmail some Democratic party officials. Thus, the Cox, Silbert, and Petersen handling of the grand jury may tell us that the integrity of the prosecutor, and not the grand jury as currently structured, was decisive on the question of whether the public interest was to be protected.

To strengthen the grand jury's independence, therefore, we should give it the authority to *initiate* investigations into criminal offenses by any officer of the government.* The grand jury theoretically has this power now, but the court that gives the jurors their instructions should be required to inform them of same. Grand jurors should also be empowered to ask the court to appoint a special attorney to substitute for the regular prosecutor if enough of their members desire such an additional measure of independence. Such a special prosecutor should be subject to discharge only by the grand jury or by the judge who authorized his appointment, when he receives evidence of serious dereliction of duty.

---

*This would be the one exception to a transfer of investigatory power to the prosecutor alone—both such a prosecutor and the grand jury could initiate such an investigation.

# CONCLUSION

One thing that seems endemic to American problem solving is that we are activated only in the midst of crises and do not anticipate and avoid them by planning, whether it be an energy crisis or unemployment brought on by a shift from a wartime to a peacetime economy. The abuses of the grand jury are no longer in a "crisis" stage, because the executive branch had all of the intense scrutiny it could stand through the accident of Watergate, but this does not mean that the possibility of an undefined and uncontrolled institution's being exploited is not still with us. The grand jury is there to be used in the same fashion by any administration, against any of its political enemies, be they from the right or the left. We are undergoing a painful period in which we must dismantle many of the myths about our country, its institutions, and our past. It is time we realize that one of our "great" institutions, the federal grand jury, is not the bulwark between tyrannical government and innocent citizens that we have mistakenly claimed it to be. If we are willing to admit this, we can go about building in the controls and protections that may yet enable the grand

jury to achieve some of the ideals that have been ascribed
to it. The correction of the institution's faults needs only a
concerned public and responsible public officials whose
memories are not too short.

Beyond the need for immediate reform of the grand
jury, one pervasive thing emerges from a study of our recent history—the grand jury was but one part of a deliberate
and calculated program to use various governmental
powers to stigmatize the Nixon administration's critics as
"criminal" by sheer force of fiat. The general lawlessness
and dictatorial perversion of power must mark (one hopes)
some exceptional low point for a national administration.
Nixon and his campaign strategists put maximum strain on
our faith in the capacity of the democratic process to allow
us to choose the "best" person for high office. Without
doubt, the high moral, even legal, costs of slick advertising
and image manipulation have become startlingly apparent.
Changing the law to bring some rein on institutions like
the grand jury is possible—but even such changes as have
been suggested here can be subverted by an unscrupulous
and callous administration. One fondly repeated saying
is that we are a "government of laws, not men," but men
must administer the laws, and *all* laws, of necessity, vest
some formal or actual latitude and discretion in the admin-
istrator. It is in the area of discretion that intention and
motive work themselves out, and those intentions must be
guided and informed by integrity and good faith for there
to be a just application of law.

The ultimate protection of our political institutions
and the public may rest on the character of the people we
elect to run them. The hardest and most ominous fact to
face is that we, the American people, had a symbiotic relationship with Richard Nixon—he tried to create the "silent
majority," but we were not completely fooled, for we

must have signaled to him that we were ready for some degree of autocratic rule if it would mean that we would all (or the "good people" at least) be more safe and secure. And so we must ask ourselves, What were we so afraid of, what were we running from with such great haste that we were ready to choose a leader with so much contempt for values we have nurtured and sought to develop since the country was created? No law can protect us from ourselves.

One can only hope that we as a people give up our adolescence (and nostalgic attempts to recapture it) and face the reality of our self-deception. Our shock and exhaustion from recent events should turn not to cynicism but to a renewed commitment to demanding high purpose and humanity from those who lead us.

# REFERENCES

## CHAPTER II.

1. A more detailed analysis of the factual background for this chapter can be found in "Demythologizing the Historic Role of the Grand Jury," H. Schwartz, 10 Am. Crim. L. Rev. 701 (1972).

2. S. Thompson and E. Merriman, *A Treatise on the Organization and Conduct of Juries, Including Grand Juries* (1882), sec. 475-476, pp. 568-569.

## CHAPTER III.

1. For an excellent account of the history of the American grand jury up to 1941, see Richard Younger, *The People's Panel* (Providence, R.I.: Brown University Press, 1963).

2. *Ibid.,* pp. 10, 20.

3. J. Somers, *The Security of Englishmen's Lives or the Trust, Power and Duty of the Grand Juries of England* (1771), p. 3; H. Care, *English Liberties or Free Born Subject's Inheritance* (Providence, 1774).

## CHAPTER IV.

1. S. Padover, ed., *The Complete Jefferson* (Washington, D.C.: Quincey Press, 1943), p. 121.

2. H. Schwartz, "Demythologizing the Historical Role of the Grand Jury," 10 Am. Crim. L. Rev., 701, 735 (1972).

3. Richard D. Younger, *The People's Panel* (Providence, R.I.: Brown University Press 1963), pp. 155-156, 163-164.

4. *The New York Times,* March 3, 14, 15, 19, 27, April 4, 1946.

## CHAPTER V.

1. "Transcripts Tell an Epic Story of How Powerful Men Reacted," *The New York Times,* May 6, 1974, p. 1, col. 2.

2. Richard Harris, *Justice, The Crisis of Law, Order and Freedom in America* (New York: E.P. Dutton, 1970), p. 96.

3. For a fascinating and thorough, albeit inconclusive, discussion of the problem, see Victor Navasky, "The Politics of Justice," *The New York Times Magazine,* May 5, 1974, p. 18.

4. See Jerome Skolnick, *The Politics of Protest—Violent Aspects of Protest and Confrontation,* staff report to the National Commission on the Causes and Prevention of Violence, pp. 21-22, for documentation of that claim (Washington D.C.: U.S. Government Printing Office), 1969.

## CHAPTER VI.

1. *The New York Times,* January 27, 1974; Baxter Smith, "FBI Memos Reveal Repression Schemes," *The Black Scholar,* April 1974, p. 43.

## CHAPTER VIII.

1. One of the earliest and best articles on the grand jury as a mechanism for compiling dossiers is Frank J. Donner and Eugene Cerruti, "The Grand Jury Network," *The Nation*, January 3, 1972, p. 5.

2. Paul Cowan, "The New Grand Jury—A Kind of Immunity That Leads to Jail," *The New York Times Magazine*, April 29, 1973.

3. From *Juris Doctor*: "Who is Guy Goodwin and why are they saying those Terrible Things about Him," by Lacey Fosburgh, p. 14, at p. 17, Jan. 1973, Vol. 3, No. 1.

4. "The Organized Crime Control Act or Its Critics: Which Threatens Civil Liberties?" McClellan, 46 *Notre Dame Lawyer* 55, 60 (1970).

## CHAPTER X.

1. *In re Kinoy*, 326 F. Supp. 400 (1971).

2. Charles Goodell, *Political Prisoners in America* (New York: Random House, 1974), p. 262.

3. *In re Russo*, 10 Crim. L. Rev. 2145 (C.D. Cal, Oct. 17, 1971).

4. Frank J. Donner and Eugene Cerruti, "The Grand Jury Network," *The Nation*, January 3, 1972, p. 5.

## CHAPTER XI.

1. L. Boudin, "The Constitutional Privilege in Operation," 12 Lawyers Guild Rev. 128 (1952).

## CHAPTER XII.

1. *M.O.R.E.—The Journalism Review,* June 1972, p. 15.

2. Press Censorship Newsletter, put out by the Reporter's Committee for the Freedom of the Press, November-December 1973, pp. 22-23.

3. *Rolling Stones Magazine,* April 26, 1973, pp. 24-25.

4. Vincent Blasi, "Newsman's Privilege: an empirical study," 70 U. Mich. L. Rev. 229 (1971).

5. *In re Tierney,* 465 F. 2d 806, 813 (5th Cir. 1972).

6. 28 C.F.R. Sec. 50.10 (1973) Regulation Citation.

7. "Newsmen's Privilege by Federal Legislation: Within Congressional Power?" R. Dixon Jr. 1, Hastings Constitutional Law Quarterly 39, 43 (1974).

## CHAPTER XIII.

1. Article I, sec. 6, U.S. Constitution.

## CHAPTER XIV.

1. *Newsweek,* August 20, 1974, p. 19.

2. Washington *Post,* September 22, 1973.

3. September 22, 1973.

4. Kuh, "Grand Jury 'Presentment': Foul Blow or Fair Play," 55 Columbia Law Review, 1103 (1955).

5. Fed. Rule of Crim. Proc. 6(c).

CHAPTER XV.

1. See T. Pluncknett, "A Concise History of the Common Law," 112 N. 1 (5th Edition 1956).

2. See Spain, "The Grand Jury Past and Present: A Survey," 2 Am. Crim. L. Q. 119, 126-42 (1964).

CHAPTER XVI.

1. 28 U.S.C. sections 1861-1862 (1970).

2. "The Espionage Statutes and Publications of Defense Information," Edgar and Schmidt, Jr., 73 Colum. L. Rev. 929 (1973).

3. "The Challenge of Crime in a Free Society—A Report by the President's Commission on Law Enforcement and Administration of Justice" (Washington, D.C.: U.S. Government Printing Office), p. 198.

4. U.S., Congress, Senate, Committee on the Judiciary, Subcommittee on Criminal Laws and Procedures, *Hearings on S. 30,* 91st Cong., 1st sess., 1969, p. 249.

5. "The Organized Crime Control Act," Senator John McClellan, 46 Notre Dame Lawyer 55, 99 (1970).

6. Crime Commission, op. cit., p. 191.

7. Ibid., p. 200.

8. Public Law 91-452.

CHAPTER XVII.

1. Robert G. Dixon, Jr., "Newsmen's Privilege by Federal Legislation: Within Congressional Power?" Hastings Constitutional Law Quarterly 39 (1974).

CHAPTER XVIII.

1. Federal Rules of Criminal Procedure 16(a).

2. Federal Rules of Criminal Procedure 6(e); *Dennis v. United States,* 384 U.S. 855 (1966).

3. See *In re Grumbles,* U.S.D.C. N.J. Crim. No. 722-71, order (1973) (unreported).


CHAPTER XIX.

1. "Ervin and Tunney Want Inquiry into Silbert's Watergate Work," *The New York Times,* May 1, 1974, p. 39, col. 6.

2. "Petersen Ties with Nixon Reportedly Led to '73 Rift," *The New York Times,* May 3, 1974, p. 1., col. 6.

# INDEX

Political activists, 4-6, 47, 134
  lawyers of, 50, 52, 57
  surveillance of, 41, 43-44,
    47-50, 73, 77, 110, 125
  trials of, 51-53, 58-65, 108-9,
    124-125
Political assassinations, 4, 36
Political corruption, 29-30, 116n,
  117, 124
Polygamy, 22
Popkin, Samuel, 67-68, 79-81
President's Commission on Law
  Enforcement and Adminis-
  tration of Justice, 114-116
Press, the, *see* Newspaper
  reporters
Princeton University, 79
Privacy, 112-113, 123
Public interest, 112, 121
Public officials, grand jury
  investigations of, 88-103,
  117, 120-121, 128-130
Public Works Committee, 88

Quakers, 112

Rangel, Charles, 125
Reconstruction, 26
Reilly, Matthias, 54
Richardson, Elliot, attorney
  generalship of, 86, 100
Riot Act, 16
Rodberg, Leonard, 88-89
Roosevelt, Franklin D., 23
Russo, Anthony, 61

St. Louis (Mo.), 30
San Francisco (Calif.), 30, 78

Schippers, David, 138
Scholars, 67-68, 73, 79-81, 93,
  128-129
Schwerner, Nathan, 60-61
Seale, Bobby, trial of, 109
Seattle (Wash.), 49, 51-52
Secrecy, 93-96, 116-117, 123-127
Sedition Act, 20
Selection of the grand jury, xii-
  xiii, 10-11, 15-16, 109
Senate Select Committee on
  Presidential Campaign
  Activities (Senate Watergate
  Committee), 28, 50, 76
Shaftsbury, 1st Earl of, 10-12, 18
Sibert, Earl J., 144-145
"Silent majority," 5, 148
Sirica, John J., xiv, 101-103, 144
Sixth Amendment, 101n
Slavery, 15, 22, 26
Smith Act, 23-24
Socialist Workers Party, 40
Solicitor general, office of, 112
Solitary confinement, 137
Soloway, Fred, 62
Somers, John, 16
*Sostre v. McGinnis*, 138n
Sources of information, 75-87
South Carolina, 14-16
Stamp Act Riots, 17
Stans, Maurice, xi, 145
State Department, 24, 91
Steiner, Daniel, 81
Students for a Democratic
  Society (SDS), 41, 48, 50
Subpoenas, 57-61, 63-66, 71, 106,
  110, 121-122, 127-129, 141-143
  of the press, 73-78, 81-83, 85-87,
  97, 130, 133
  of public officials, 89, 120n, 130
  of scholars, 79-80